BOB M^CCABE THE EXORCIST

OMNIBUS PRESS
London / New York / Sydney

ISBN: 0 7119 7509 4
Order No: OP 48103

Exclusive Distributors
Book Sales Limited,
8/9 Frith Street
London W1V 5TZ, UK.

The Five Mile Press,
22 Summit Road
Noble Park
Victoria 3174, Australia.

To the Music Trade only:
Music Sales Limited,
8/9 Frith Street
London W1V 5TZ, UK.

A catalogue record for this book is available from the British Library.

Visit Omnibus Press at http://www.musicsales.co.uk

The publishers are grateful to the follwing agewncies for the use of photographs in this book : Camera Press, Hulton Getty, The Ronald Grant Archive, The Kobal Collection, Moviestore Collection, Pictorial Press, Rex Features

The author and publishers have made every reasonable effort to contact the copyright holders of the photographs in this book. Any errors that may have occurred are inadvertent and anyone who for any reason has not been contacted is invited to write to the publishers so that a full acknowledgment may be made in subsequent editions of this work.

DEDICATION

For Mark, Alan and Nigel –
honourable men in an increasingly tawdry world.

ACKNOWLEDGEMENTS

A couch, somewhere in Harrow, circa 1974.

So this is how it begins: it's a Sunday night and dark outside. A young boy, maybe eight years old or so, sits on a couch, his mother beside him. The lights are out; in fact the only light in the room comes from the black-and-white box in the corner which is currently offering nothing but adverts. And then it happens – a man, all in black, steps out of a car, and stands silhouetted before a large imposing house, briefcase in hand. He has the potential to be the most terrifying *unknown* this young boy has ever encountered. From the box comes a voice, deep and as creepy as you'd expect. It says something along the lines of "Finally, *The Exorcist* has arrived in Britain." The boy half turns to his mother, afraid to take his eyes off the screen in case something else happens, in case it gets him. Then he asks her, "Mum, what's an Exorcist?". She answers "It's someone who's come to fight the Devil." The boy is rooted to the spot. After eight years of forced Sunday evening trips to the local Catholic church, this has an impact and he thinks to himself, "You mean, all that stuff is real?". It is probably the most genuinely terrifying moment this boy will ever have. He doesn't sleep a wink that night. . .

Only years later does it all make sense. The one element that was missing from the loop becomes clear; my mother thought I realised it was a movie – that she was explaining the plot to a film. I didn't have a bloody clue that what I was watching wasn't real and this is how fear begins. . . .

When I set out to write this book, I thought it would be a definitive look at the making of what probably remains the most terrifying film ever made. It's ended up being something quite different to that. What follows is, in many ways, an oral history of *The Exorcist* – the book, the film, the enduring phenomenon. In talking to many of those directly involved in the film, what I found was how much of the stuff of legends the film had become. Billy Friedkin would insist a story was one way, Linda Blair another. The further I looked into the story of *The Exorcist*, the more I realised how many tales there were.

But that was just as it should be, because this was always a movie about stories. People who queued for hours to see the movie didn't just go for the movie; they went to see if the other stories were true, to see if they would throw up or pass out, or have a heart attack. Better still, they went to see if this would happen to the person next to them so that they could go and tell their friends about it.

If ever a movie was inextricably linked to the stories it generated, both during production (the so-called 'curse' of *The Exorcist*) and on its release, then it is this one. What this book aims to do is to put all that information together in one place, and let the reader judge for himself. Our pre-millennial mantra seems to be the *X Files*-inspired 'The truth is out there'. Well, the truth is in here, *somewhere* – you just have to search through the hype, the lies and the insanity that surrounded this unique movie to find it. Which is the way it should be.

The week that I finished writing this book, *The Exorcist* opened in the UK to mark its twenty-fifth anniversary. In its first weekend it took over £2 million and became the number one film in the country, a quarter-century after it last achieved this. I think I might be onto something.

There are, as ever, more thank yous than a Sally Field Oscar speech (in theory, a thing of the past, I'm glad to say). First and foremost, I am hugely indebted to the good doctor Mark Kermode, the world's leading *Exorcist* scholar, whose *BFI Modern Classic* on the movie remains the definitive reading of the film. I must thank Mark for his time, patience, yards of advice, phone book, archive access and, above all else, his valued friendship. Many of the original articles sourced and at times quoted in this book were written by Dr. Kermode in publications as diverse as *Fangoria* and *Sight and Sound*. I am additionally hugely indebted to Mark for allowing me access to more than forty hours of interviews he conducted for the BBC documentary *The Fear of God*, the majority of which remain unseen. Much of the quoted material from Fathers Bermingham and O'Malley, Jason Miller, Linda Blair and Max von Sydow that appear in this book are sourced from Mark's original interviews for the BBC, without which this book would not have been possible. Or at least it would have been considerably shorter. (Ellen Burstyn also appears – largely – courtesy of *The Fear of God*.) Special thanks also to Mark's wife, Linda Ruth Williams for putting up with us and I'll take this opportunity to offer them extreme congratulations on the birth of their first daughter Georgia, who showed up at more or less the same time as this manuscript (and yes, she was late as well!).

Alan Jones of the 'Alan Jones Collection' was, as ever, a huge help in the writing of this tome, as was Rob Churchill, who constantly asked me to explain the plot of *Exorcist II* to him (something I have yet to do satisfactorily).

Thanks to Ian Nathan and Adam Smith at *Empire* magazine for their help in the article that sparked this book and to Jane Trotman at Warners for her excellent assistance with arranging the initial interviews. And of course, much gratitude to Mal Peachey, John Conway and all at Essential for all their tireless work, dedication, blah, blah, blah.

Of the people behind *The Exorcist*, I am deeply indebted to both Bill Blatty and Billy Friedkin for allowing me to take up far too much of their time and to test their patience. Both men were warm, generous and, above all else, fine storytellers. Gentlemen, I salute you. (A brief aside: when I went out to LA to interview Friedkin and Blatty, I flew on a Virgin plane named Tubular Belle. My plane reading was Blatty's *Demons Five, Exorcists Nothing*, in which the central character has an office near the Farmer's Market district of LA, opposite the CBS building. When I got to the motel I was staying at – which had been booked for me by a friend – I found myself facing the Farmer's Market and the CBS building. When dealing with a subject like *The Exorcist*, I think you should take all the good omens you can get!) Additional thanks to the extremely courteous Dick Smith, Linda Blair, Jason Miller, Max von Sydow, Bryan Michael Stoller and others.

Acknowledgements

I must also thank Nick Freand Jones, late of the BBC and now at Channel 4 for access around and about his fine documentary *The Fear of God*.

Love and thanks as always to Mary McCabe. And finally, as always, this book was made possible by the participation, patience, love and support of Lucy Merritt and Jessie McCabe. In what has been a ridiculously hectic time, I owe them vast amounts of love and vast amounts of everything else.

Bob McCabe, November 1998

CONTENTS

CHAPTER ONE

1949

In 1949, in the Mount Rainier district of Maryland, a young boy was said to be possessed by the Devil. The news made the papers and caused a sensation. It first appeared as a small piece in the *Catholic Review* in Washington, the child's symptoms having been presented before the Washington Society of Parapsychology. Although the names of both the boy in question and the priest who was said to have performed the exorcism ritual were never revealed, the case was also briefly reported in the *Washington Daily News*. On 20 August of that year, Bill Brinkley wrote as detailed an account as possible in the *Washington Post*, the newspaper that, a quarter of a century later on, would be instrumental in bringing down President Richard Nixon.

Brinkley's piece began: 'In what is perhaps one of the most remarkable experiences of its kind in recent religious history, a 14-year-old Mount Rainier boy has been freed by a Catholic priest of possession of the Devil, Catholic sources reported yesterday.' The journalist went on to reveal that the boy had been subjected to up to thirty readings of the ancient Roman Ritual of exorcism, during which he continually 'broke into a violent tantrum of screaming, cursing and voicing of Latin phrases – a language he had never studied – whenever the priest reached those climactic points of the 27-page ritual in which he commanded the demon to depart from the boy.'

Father Merrin (Max von Sydow)

The priest stayed with the boy for over two months, moving between St Louis and Washington, during which time he witnessed a variety of paranormal phenomena, including the sudden movement across the room of the boy's sturdy cot-bed, with the boy on top of it. Since the final exorcism, performed in May, the boy had suffered no further manifestations.

Brinkley's piece went on to explain that before resorting to the act of exorcism, the boy had been subjected to a barrage of medical and psychiatric tests, many of which had been performed at Georgetown University Hospital, a Jesuit institution. The priest prepared himself by fasting and then performed the Roman Ritual. During each recitation the boy reacted violently at the passages in which the priest ordered the evil spirit to leave the child's body. What little information was revealed about the family in question included the facts that the boy's father was a mechanic and that both parents were non-Catholics who had sought the help of the Catholic church, having initially turned to their Lutheran minister for help. The minister had taken the boy into his own home where he also experienced a number of paranormal incidents.

In a later interview with the *Washington Star*, Father John Nicola, assistant director of the National Catholic Shrine of the Immaculate Conception in Washington (and an adviser on *The Exorcist* film), described various elements of the case: "In school it was the same. His desk moved around the floor of the classroom as if it were on wheels; the other children became disturbed and soon the boy had to be taken out of school. Then came the nightmares and the boy would wake up screaming. A chest of drawers weighing 70 or 80 pounds moved across the room with the drawers opening and closing. . . . There were brief periods of recession, but there were other signs. Branding would appear on his body, from which blood would flow."

'Use of the ritual is rare in the Western Christian world,' Brinkley concluded in his report, 'as are reported cases of diabolical possession. Never is permission to employ the ritual granted except where an afflicted person's case has been fully documented as being a bona fide one.'

The priest who performed the exorcism was later revealed to be one Father William S. Bowdern. He was assisted in the ritual by Fathers Raymond J. Bishop and Walter Halloran.

Many people read the *Washington Post*'s report of the case; amongst them was a twenty-year-old student at the Jesuit-run Georgetown University named William Peter Blatty. "I was a Georgetown student carrying thirty-one hours and two majors – one in English and one in philosophy," Blatty recalls today. "Nobody had time, nor did I have the money, to read newspapers. So I got it [the news of the exorcism] in class. It was the first one I ever heard about. Apparently the exorcism was going on at that time, contemporaneously with this class in which I heard about it, and the exorcist must have been temporarily billeted at the campus. And that's where all these stories were coming from – from the happy hour before dinner – stories were exchanged. And that's where I heard about it. Of course, I heard things that in later years I realised were wildly exaggerated, details about the boy speaking fluently in Latin were not quite accurate, and there were details of the copy of the Roman Ritual the exorcist held in his hand at one point suddenly exploding. None of that happened. But there were unbelievably mystifying paranormal phenomena, enough to get my attention."

As all good Catholic boys must, in order to become good Catholic men, Blatty was undergoing something of a crisis of faith. The possession of a contemporary was, in an unexpected way, good news for him. Surely it was proof that God existed. If the Devil (or his minion) had indeed been proven to have been within that boy, then surely the existence of such evil must lead to an acceptance of the reality of good? "At the time," says Blatty "I thought, wouldn't it be wonderful? Because I had always had struggles with my faith, mostly out of fear that it might not be true, which terrified me."

Blatty had already entered an oratorical contest on campus, but with one day to go, he still didn't have a subject to discuss. His one-time tutor from his Brooklyn prep school, Father Thomas Bermingham S. J., was in town at the time. The two men had become fast friends and Bermingham had noticed a story in the paper that might be appropriate for Blatty's approaching discourse. "Coming through Union Station I just happened to pick up a newspaper to read while I was in the City," Father Bermingham recounted during the making of the documentary *The Fear Of God* . "And when I got to Georgetown, Mr Blatty was in something of a panic. He had signed up for an oratorical contest, which was very popular in those days, but he didn't have a speech yet. So I said, 'Bill, let's see what's in the headlines. We'll get something that nobody is doing.' And sure enough, the headline in every paper in Washington was an apparent case of Satanic possession. And we got together, worked a speech out, and the next night he won the contest."

"I thought, well, my God, if this could be researched and written about, and some of these details could be corroborated," says Blatty, "it would seem to substantiate certainly the existence of intelligences that can survive without a body, namely spirits. And if bad spirits, why not good? But at any rate it would certainly suggest the possibility of God and definitely suggest the probability of some form of after-life."

The seed was planted; it would take twenty years to come to fruition.

WILLIAM PETER BLATTY

Religion has always played a big part in the life of Bill Blatty. His great uncle, Germanios Mouakad, was the foremost theologian and philosopher in the Middle East in his day, having founded a mission, the Society of St. Paul, in the Lebanon. Bill's American-based descendants were brought up to be Roman Catholic. Born 7 January 1928 in New York City, young Bill attended St Stephen's Catholic Grammar School in New York, followed by Brooklyn Preparatory, a Jesuit high school, where he was taught by Father Thomas Bermingham. He then went on to Georgetown University, also a Jesuit school, on scholarship with financial contributions from his Lebanese mother, who made and packaged her own quince jelly, selling it on the streets of New York, often outside the Plaza Hotel. Bill had, naturally, entertained thoughts of becoming a priest, but instead he found that his post-college life led him into a variety of jobs, including driving beer trucks and selling vacuum cleaners from door-to-door. He also spent some time based in the Middle East with the United States Information Service, where he analysed Soviet propaganda for the US Air Force. This was followed by a stint as publicity director for the University of Southern California and Loyola University.

Bill first discovered his talent for writing at the age of ten when he won $5 in a twenty-five-words-or-less caption contest for *Captain*

Future comic books. He was further inspired as an adolescent by a short story by Robert Bloch entitled *Time Wounds All Heels*. "I just fell about with laughter," Blatty has said. "I would call my friends and read the entire story to them. And I caught fire. I wanted to write something like that."

Having joined the Information Service in 1951, Blatty achieved his wish when he penned a series of comic articles for the *Saturday Evening Post*, detailing his experiences in the Middle East. These pieces formed the basis of his first book *Which Way To Mecca, Jack?* published in 1959. After winning $5,000 as a contestant on Groucho Marx's quiz show *You Bet Your Life*, Blatty quit his job at Loyola University and concentrated on full-time writing. His second novel *John Goldfarb, Please Come Home* was published shortly afterwards. Both books were funny, satirical pieces and led to Blatty landing a job as a screenwriter in Hollywood. His first screenplay, the Danny Kaye vehicle, *The Man From The Diner's Club*, was produced in 1963 and led to a lucrative career working as a comedy writer, often in collaboration with director Blake Edwards, for whom Blatty penned the Pink Panther sequel *A Shot In The Dark* amongst others. "Normally comic novels took a couple of months to write," says Blatty. "A script sometimes a few weeks. I not only wrote comedy but I was a specialist in the wild farce, off-the-wall kind of material."

It was whilst he was working with Edwards on a project – *Gunn*, a spin-off from Edwards' *Peter Gunn TV Show* – that Blatty first encountered a young director named William Friedkin. "I recall very vividly Billy Friedkin was critical of only one thing in the screenplay and it was a dream sequence which, as it happened, I had written. And I said nothing about it but Blake, rather forcibly, defended it. And Friedkin would not back off. He just kept arguing and arguing that it was not acceptable, it was not in keeping with the texture of the rest of the film, and so on. And I thought to myself, he's not going to get this job; he must know that. He must know he's ruining whatever chances he had." Needless to say, Friedkin didn't get the job.

Blatty, meanwhile, was eager to look beyond the limitations of slapstick. "I had always carried with me the desire to write some version of an account of an exorcism in a way that would make it credible for people and, forgive me for sounding semi-idealistic, I wanted to give people hope and stimulate their religious beliefs. . . . But of course, I was terrified of my ability to write something that wasn't comedic. I had no idea if I was capable of it, and I was daunted by the amount of time it would take."

As early as 1963 Blatty had attempted to do just this, but both his agent and his publisher at the time were against the idea. So he continued with comedy until the bottom dropped out of the market. Hollywood in the late sixties was a desperate place to be. The huge (and unexpected) success of *The Graduate* radically redefined what the studios thought its audience wanted to see. A whole new, younger audience was obviously eager for a different kind of product. Blake Edwards' knockabouts simply weren't doing it for them anymore.

"Motion picture comedies were out of favour, at least in Hollywood, and I could not convince anybody to hire me for a project that wasn't comedy," Blatty recalls. "Even if it was something where priests were the protagonist – 'Oh, I have a very heavy religious background' – no, no, no. And I thought well, as I have nothing better to do now than go down to the unemployment office and pick up my cheque, this is the perfect time to write. And so I began."

William Peter Blatty: Filmography Pre- *Exorcist*
(As screenwriter unless otherwise stated)
The Man From The Diner's Club (1963 – also co-story)
A Shot In The Dark (1964)
John Goldfarb, Please Come Home (1965 – from his own novel)
Promise Her Anything (1966)
What Did You Do In The War, Daddy? (1966)
Gunn (1967)
The Great Bank Robbery (1969)
Darling Lili (1970)
The Exorcist (1973 – from his own novel, also producer)

THE NOVEL

Blatty had at first hoped that any book that was to be written
stemming from the 1949 Mount Rainier case would be a factual
one. He managed to make contact with Father Bowdern to offer his
assistance with just such a work. "I tracked down Father Eugene
Gallagher, from whom I had heard about the case, and he gave me
the name of the exorcist. And I found him at St Louis University and I
wrote to him. And he first wrote back to me to say he was quite
anxious to help but he was going to go to the Bishop, to whom he
had originally promised complete confidentiality. The family wanted
nothing at all ever, ever to be made public about this case, which
stimulated my belief in the possibility that this might be real. But he
wrote back to me that the Archbishop and the Cardinal had said no.
The family wanted no part of it, they wanted no book written, no
account, nothing. And so I got another letter back saying 'Sorry
about this, but the one thing I can tell you is the case I was involved
with was the real thing. I had no doubts about it then; I have no doubt
about it now.' Well that electrified me; that was enough to start me
off. I made one more effort to get him to go back to the Cardinal to
say: 'Look, this is a non-fiction book and we're going to change all
the names, and it'll be written by you, Father. I'll help you, I'll edit.'
But the answer was still no."

So Blatty decided to novelise the story. He began his research by looking into other incidents of reported exorcism. "But you couldn't find anyone who had ever been involved with an exorcism," he says. "In the United States, I could only find three instances in which the Catholic church had given its express and explicit approval for a form of exorcism to be conducted. The 1949 case was one, then there was one in 1928 in Earling, Iowa, and the third one was only rumoured, possibly in Cleveland in 1962. I never could find anything on that. I found the material on the case in Iowa, but unfortunately all of the participants were deceased. And I was left with this account which struck me as having been written by an overly credulous person, so that was absolutely useless to me. But it was clear to me that something called possession was going on and was real."

Throughout the years, Blatty had kept in touch with his mentor, Father Bermingham. "He finally ended up in Hollywood doing work in farces," Father Bermingham once explained to the BBC. "Above all was his famous Peter Sellers film (*A Shot In The Dark*) which is not exactly my favourite type of entertainment. And I once told him that if he didn't do something more with his talent, I would never give him an 'A', only a 'B'. And after one of his films would come out, I would get a telegram saying 'Do I get an A?' And I said 'No, a B.'

"On one occasion I was attending an education convention in Hollywood and he took me out to dinner and for the first time I felt he was getting a bit angry with me. And he literally said 'What the hell do you want me to do?' And I said 'You know Bill, I have a growing feeling that we don't face up to the full dimensions of the problem of evil.' And he said 'Do you remember that case in Maryland of the satanic possession?' And I had forgotten it completely, hadn't thought about it. But it had lodged in his imagination and he said 'I'd like to do something along those lines'. He was stubborn and I have always felt that you don't fool around with an artist with imagination. I said 'I'll work with you on one condition – that you take it seriously. I don't want another *Rosemary's Baby*. I want somebody that really will confront this in a serious way. And you have to study it for a year because, as you know Bill, it's the single greatest problem that Jews and Christians are confronted with – the awesome problem of the evil in God's world. So we worked for a year before he wrote the first page."

At one point, Blatty toyed with the idea of writing the story as a screenplay instead of a novel. "As a matter of fact it was on the night that my mother died. At about 8 o'clock at night, I started writing a screenplay version because I couldn't interest anybody in publishing a novel. And I thought, well, scripts are easier than books, let me try it now and see if I can finish it. And I'd typed about a page and half of it and the phone rang to tell me my mother had died, and I never went back to it."

Blatty once claimed that it was a sign from his dead mother that convinced him to carry on with the book. He was writing in a cabin in Lake Tahoe. "But I wasn't able to get the novel going. So I took off for a few days to drive to a nearby lodge for a sauna. When I walked into the steam room, I was wearing a Jesuit medal on a single chain around my neck." Blatty had worn the medal for many years but when he awoke the next morning he found two chains and two medals around his neck. "The second one was a coppery Immaculate Conception medal, old and worn smooth, exactly like the one my mother had always worn around her neck. To this day there is no explanation of how the medal could have gotten there. I was alone so it couldn't have been put there in my sleep by someone. I knew instantly that my mother was trying to tell me I was on the right track – to get back to writing the book."

At a New Year's Eve party at the home of the novelist Burton Wohl, Blatty met Mark Jaffe, an editorial director at Bantam Books. Over dinner, Jaffe asked Blatty what he was working on. At that stage Blatty had little more than the subject matter, some sketchy characters and the barest bones of a possible plot. But Jaffe was intrigued enough by the possibilities of the story and the notion of possession to suggest that Bantam might well want to publish it, and offered Blatty a sizeable advance. This was enough to get the author going, finally finding form to a tale that had been building up inside him for the best part of two decades.

In his first correspondence with Jaffe, Blatty detailed many of the events of the 1949 incident and the Catholic church's stance on possession. At that point the story still dealt with a possessed boy, while the exorcist was named Father Thomas, in reference to his old tutor Father Thomas Bermingham. The character of the atheist mother, eventually called Chris MacNeil, was based in part on Blatty's neighbour of the time, actress Shirley MacLaine.

"I had never written a serious female character and I didn't know if I could do it. So I cast about for a model and I knew Shirley rather well and she was absolutely perfect. She had this down home plain quality, not to say she isn't a very intelligent woman. But she's from Missouri. She's someone who would be extremely sceptical of some tale of possession and the last person you would expect to have a possessed child."

"Of course I was Chris MacNeil," MacLaine confided to Friedkin biographer Nat Segaloff. "Bill used the French couple who ran my house in the book. He used J. Lee Thompson [the British director who was widely believed to be the model for Burke Dennings] as the basis for the director, and the first seance I ever went to, he arranged in my house."

Blatty's research continued in search of a story. At first, he seems to have mistrusted his instincts, taking his knowledge and themes, and then converting them into a murder mystery story. "That was the version that I offered to Bantam books," he recalls. "It was a murder mystery and it became a courtroom kind of a book where the defence offered was possession. And that would be the vehicle to explore the reality of possession and credibility, and so on. I got off that when I got another letter from the exorcist because that would have been a very easy way to go. It was only ever in a letter outlining what I proposed to do to the publisher; it was never written."

Over the next nine months, Blatty worked up to fourteen hours a day writing *The Exorcist*. When it was finally finished, he took a xerox copy round to his neighbour, Ms MacLaine, who was so impressed that she quickly suggested turning the novel into a movie, with herself lined up to star. Blatty agreed in theory, provided that he could produce the movie as well, but a satisfactory deal could not be worked out in time and MacLaine, still intrigued with the concept of possession, went off to make the far inferior – and now forgotten – *The Possession Of Joel Delaney*.

The relationship between Blatty and MacLaine was further strained when journalists, picking up on MacLaine as being the inspiration for Chris MacNeil, went so far as to posit that the story was, in fact, a true tale, based on MacLaine's daughter Stephanie Scahiko ('Sachi'). MacLaine herself insists that the distorted image on the first hardback printing of the novel was, in fact, a picture of her daughter that was taken by Blatty. "He still claims that the picture on the front of *The Exorcist* is not my daughter, Sachi," the actress told Segaloff. "But it is. He took it himself and distorted it photographically. Her friends used to ask her about it."

(As the success of the book grew, MacLaine became so annoyed at the unintentional and unwanted attention its notoriety brought to her that she contemplated suing Blatty, but eventually took the action no further.)

Harper & Row won the bidding war that followed for the hardback rights to the novel which appeared in 1971, to little or no sales. "I always expected that it would be respectfully received," says Blatty. "That was the height of my ambition for it, that it be respectably received and that I don't get any notices that said Blatty should stick to comedy. Those were my highest ambitions. That it was well received did not surprise me. By the time I was about three quarters of the way through it, I had the feeling that it could be very popular. But, as a matter of fact, when it was first put out no one was reading it. Book stores were returning it by the car load. I went out on a promotional tour for Harper & Row and I remember I'd get off airplanes and be greeted by the Harper rep saying 'Well, the May company returned ninety-nine out of one hundred copies.' I had one very poignant little episode – in New York City the Harper rep took me over to one store to autograph copies and this girl in the store said I was forbidden to sign them because then they couldn't return them. I was crushed. There was a store in Los Angeles where they were selling, but that was an isolated phenomenon."

An opportunity to appear on Dick Cavett's popular daytime talk show proved to be the turning point for *The Exorcist*. "I had a pre-interview for the show and the young lady that interviewed me told me it was a long shot, that Cavett is not into this kind of thing, thank you for coming. And at lunch I got a call from Harper & Row saying one of the guests on the Cavett show was ill and could not appear. And they had apparently tried maybe thirty other people and they couldn't reach any of them. But they found me. So I raced over there and got into make-up, and I was slated to go on in the author's slot, which was the last five minutes or so of the show. But somebody was watching over me. The first guest was found to be boring and got the hook after one segment. The second guest was not only boring but a little inebriated and he got the hook. There was nobody left but me. And I came out and Cavett had forty-five minutes to fill and he did the most wonderful thing. He said 'Mr Blatty, to be honest with you, I have not read your book.' So I said: 'Well, may I tell you about it?' Well, I got to do virtually a monologue interrupted only by commercials. And the day I left Manhattan I picked up *Time* magazine and I got to the book section and I saw *The Exorcist* was number four on the bestsellers list."

Early on, Blatty had begun negotiating film rights with producer Paul Monash. Monash optioned the book and had six months to set the deal up, with himself attached as executive producer and Blatty on board as producer. Warner Brothers quickly picked up the film, although by then Blatty and Monash were having numerous disagreements. Monash wanted to move the location from Washington, change Chris MacNeil's career, lose the Iraq-set prologue, change the characterisation of Kinderman (probably the character to whom Blatty was most strongly attached) and drop Merrin completely. Quickly, Blatty arranged for Warner's to buy Monash out, leaving him as sole producer. His fee for the movie sale was reportedly $641,000 plus 35.1 per cent of the profits. It was a good deal better than the Bantam advance that he had struggled to live on for the last year.

Blatty knew from experience that turning producer was the only way to ensure that his material could be protected. "The first film I ever wrote was a Danny Kaye comedy called *The Man From The Diners' Club* and the prospective director, who had done a lot of Red Skelton movies, came into the producer's office waving the script and saying 'I've got to have this, I've got to do this, I need a hit and this is it.' But the moment the contract was signed, he started changing it."

Undoubtedly one of the great strengths of Blatty's novel, and one of the keys to its success, lay in his expert juxtaposition between the real and the unfathomable. Blatty's book was never a tale of shock and excess. Despite the use of graphically strong language and such vividly unnerving moments as the twelve-year-old Regan masturbating with a crucifix (surely the first time anywhere, in the mainstream, such a potent religious symbol had been forced into physical and, more importantly, intellectual contact with the female vagina), *The Exorcist* set out to present the mysteries of faith in a rational world. Chris MacNeil is at pains to explore all that the scientific world has to offer in finding a 'cure' for her daughter; Blatty is at pains to notate and detail all the possible interpretations of Regan's manifest 'illness', listing literally scores of reference books (which Blatty himself laboriously pored over), that firmly root his tale of the extraordinary in the real world of the day. Indeed, his key religious character, Father Karras, was a man with a foot in both worlds, a priest and a psychiatrist. Not only that, but a priest who had lost his faith but still had a firm belief in his science, to the point where even he could rationalise Regan's 'possession' as being something other than demonic. Only by exhausting every legitimate alternative – both physiological and psychological – can Chris MacNeil, the post-sixties, defiantly and appropriately atheist mother, look beyond her understanding, put her logic and rationale aside, and take a leap of faith. Blatty asked nothing of his readers that his characters didn't have to undergo first.

It was a unique approach that touched a nerve with a generation of readers, who had witnessed the harsh reality of Vietnam and would soon discover the false piety of leaders, courtesy of Watergate. For all of its paranormal moments, *The Exorcist* was, ironically, a work of realism. Only by getting that aspect right, could the rest of the novel work. Blatty knew this was also intrinsic to the success of a movie made from the book. He knew that he needed the right man in his corner. He went for a documentarian, who was also displaying a neat line in narrative and genre-defining car chases. "It wasn't that I wanted to be a producer but the chief way of protecting it (the movie) was the selection of the director and my first choice was Friedkin. But they didn't want him."

WILLIAM FRIEDKIN

William Friedkin was born on 29 August 1935 in Chicago. His mother was a nurse and his father worked for his older brothers in a chain of discount clothing stores for men. As a child he was a keen and decent enough basketball player.

His parents couldn't afford to send him to college, which was fine with Billy, who instead began his professional career at the age of sixteen by working in the mail room of his local Chicago TV station WGN-TV. "The station was owned by the *Chicago Tribune* then," Friedkin recollects, "and I worked in the mail room for close to a year, and then I was promoted to what they call a floor manager, which is equivalent to an assistant director in film. I did that for about a year and a half. Then I was promoted to director of live television programmes. But that was not uncommon. I had no college, no university, that's how guys advanced. They either worked as an usher for a television network or they started in the mail room of a station and you could work your way up. There were really no film schools of any significance then and if there had been, I wouldn't have gone to one because I didn't like the educational process. It was a way to start a career in broadcasting in those days. And I know that the path that I took is somewhat unique. I don't think it could be duplicated today. With the proliferation of film schools, why should someone go to work in the mail room, you know?"

In Chicago, Friedkin directed over 2,000 hours of live television. "I directed about eight or nine live shows a day, every day for eight years. So just add that up. Everything from news to kids shows like *Bozo's Circus* and *Lunchtime Little Theatre*, chat shows, dramatic shows. I did a show called *They Stand Accused*, which was the first live courtroom drama, on the old Dumont Network. Musical programmes – the Chicago Symphony Orchestra, baseball games, all of it live."

At the time, Friedkin never gave movies a second thought, being content to remain working within live television. Then one fateful afternoon he went to a matinee screening of *Citizen Kane* at the Surf theatre, a local arthouse in Chicago. "And then I stayed and watched it two or three more times that same day. And it was at that point – I was still in my twenties – that I determined to try and direct film."

Friedkin decided that the way into movies would come from directing documentaries for the local Chicago stations, something they had never done before. *WGN* passed on the idea so Friedkin jacked in his job there and moved to the station's competitors, *WBKB*. Here, in 1962, he made *The People Versus Paul Crump*, a portrait of a convict convicted of killing a guard during a baby food factory hold-up. Crump was on death row but he insisted that he was innocent. The film showed that, even as a documentarian, Friedkin would go to any lengths to make the movie he wanted.

"He [Crump] was telling a story to the camera of how the police beat a confession out of him. When he told me the story when I first heard it in his prison cell, of how the police beat him and made him confess to a crime he didn't commit, he broke down in tears. Then I put a camera in his face with lights and shit – nothing. So I slapped this guy who was on death row for murder. He was about to go to the electric chair, and I slapped him in the face to surprise him and then said 'OK, *now* tell me the story.' And it was not simply the physical act of the slap, it was the thing that is, in effect, the betrayal of a friend which caused him to lose it while he was telling the story."

Friedkin's film proved too strong for television but quickly became a film festival favourite, picking up the Golden Gate Award at the San Francisco Film Festival and bringing Friedkin to the attention of TV network producer David L. Wolper, who hired him to make three documentaries for the ABC network. Friedkin left Chicago for Hollywood in 1965. He quickly moved on from working with Wolper and one of his earliest subsequent assignments was directing *Off Season*, the last ever episode of *The Alfred Hitchcock Hour*. Hitchcock showed up on set to film his customary introduction to the episode and offered Friedkin a word of advice – he told him that directors on his show usually wore ties!

"The man who was the producer of *The Alfred Hitchcock Hour* then – Norman Lloyd, who's an actor who had worked with Hitchcock – he had seen *The People Versus Paul Crump* and he thought it had more suspense in the first five minutes than any of the shows they had done all season. So he gave me a shot to direct the Hitchcock hour. That was the first thing I had ever done on a soundstage. I met Hitchcock; there's not too much to tell about that. Hitchcock was much too self-involved and self-centred to ever mentor anyone. My opinion was that if he saw any young person of genuine talent, his tendency was to shun that person and regard him as a future enemy."

Friedkin made his movie debut in 1967 with *Good Times*, a fairly forgettable vehicle for the pop duo Sonny & Cher. This was followed, in 1968, by an adaptation of Harold Pinter's *The Birthday Party*, shot in England. 1969's $5 million-budgeted *The Night They Raided Minsky's* proved to be another thematic and stylistic departure for the nascent filmmaker, with Jason Robards and British screen comic Norman Wisdom embroiled in an uneven look at the last, dying days of burlesque. For his 1970 effort Friedkin went back to the stage for inspiration, adapting playwright Mark Crowley's acclaimed *The Boys In The Band*.

These movies raised some critical eyes, and some minor box office returns, but Friedkin knew that he still hadn't managed to find what he was looking for in film. "I think they're all worthless, with the possible exception of *The Boys In The Band* which is a wonderful screenplay from a wonderful play," he says now. "Both funny and quite moving, and I was fortunate to be offered and able to make that piece of material. *The Birthday Party* is not a very cinematic piece of material. *The Night They Raided Minsky's* is a kind of a mess in which many hands took part, and the Sonny & Cher film I made is really not worth mentioning. I did it to become a film director."

By now Friedkin was dating Kitty Hawks, daughter of the legendary filmmaker Howard Hawks, and living with her in New York. A chance comment at a meeting with Hawks Sr. was to have a profound effect on the young filmmaker. The aged Hawks questioned why Friedkin would want to waste his time on something like *The Boys In The Band*. He should be making good, solid pictures with plenty of action instead. "I had this epiphany," Friedkin explained to Peter Biskind in his book *Easy Riders, Raging Bulls* "that what we were doing wasn't making fucking films to hang in the Louvre. We were making films to entertain people and if they didn't do that first, they didn't fulfil their primary purpose. It's like somebody gives you a key and you didn't know there was a lock."

That key led to *The French Connection*. The style Friedkin was searching for came together in this gritty police thriller which was based, in part, on the real life exploits of cop Eddie Egan. *The French Connection* allowed Friedkin to blend his documentary training with a compulsive storyline and characters. "Here, I felt I could impose a kind of documentary quality on fictional material, since most documentaries are a kind of fiction anyway. They all represent someone's point of view. Any time you put a camera some place, you're making an editorial comment. It's inescapable. And then how you edit the material and how you shape it. I won't say that it's distorted but it's subjective. So I had had training doing that."

The French Connection was shot for five weeks, on location in New York over the Christmas period of 1970, on a budget of $1.8 million. It was the producer Phillip D'Antoni, who had earlier produced the Steve McQueen vehicle, *Bullitt*, who insisted that the film should have a car chase. Friedkin's innovative, adrenaline-charged chase between a car and an elevated subway train not only became the defining image of the movie, but remains one of the most visceral, exciting chase sequences in all of modern cinema.

Released in October 1971, *The French Connection* was honoured with a Best Picture Academy Award and Billy Friedkin walked away with the Oscar for Best Director, the youngest director ever to win such an award.

By 1972, Francis Ford Coppola (courtesy of *The Godfather*), Peter Bogdanovich (by way of *The Last Picture Show*) and Billy Friedkin (with *The French Connection*) were the three hottest directors on the planet. They decided to set up shop together. The Directors Company would allow them to make the films they wanted to make without studio interference (if they stayed within budgetary guidelines) and to share in the profits from each other's successes. It was idealistic to say the least and doomed to failure almost from the beginning. The company's first movie was Coppola's *The Conversation*, a brilliant labyrinthine cinematic dose of paranoia that made nothing at the box office. Bogdanovich was up next and delivered the very successful *Paper Moon*. Billy and Francis took a hefty share of the profits, much to Bogdanovich's chagrin. Friedkin had yet to make a film and Coppola's had flopped. By the time Bogdanovich announced his next picture – *Daisy Miller* starring his then girlfriend and all round muse Cybil Shepherd – Friedkin wanted out. He had no intention of making what he saw as vanity pictures. Friedkin wanted to make commercial movies. Besides, he had a project already lined up at Warner Brothers. He was going to make *The Exorcist*.

William Friedkin: Filmography Pre-*Exorcist*
Good Times (1967)
The Birthday Party (1968)
The Night They Raided Minsky's (1968)
The Boys In The Band (1970)
The French Connection (1971)
The Exorcist (1973)

BILL & BILLY

"**B**ill Blatty sent the book to me before I left for a promotion tour on *The French Connection*," Friedkin says. "I didn't read it right away. I took it with me on this tour and for a couple of cities it just sat in a suitcase. And then I opened it when I was in San Francisco one evening. I was gonna go out to dinner with some people and, while I was waiting, I opened this book and I started to read it. I cancelled the dinner. I stayed in the rest of that night and finished it. And it was, of course, mesmerising. And I called Bill the next day. I knew him socially and I said 'What the hell is this?'. And he started to tell me the background to the book and that he was planning to produce a film of it and that he wanted me to direct it. And I said 'Absolutely.' It's an amazing, wonderful piece of work, highly original, unique, terrifying, profound, all of that good stuff. So he then set about to see to it that I became director of it."

"I had not seen *The French Connection* at that point," continues Blatty. "But I remembered him from the Gunn incident and he was known as a documentary filmmaker before that. And when the time came to find a director for *The Exorcist*, I thought of Friedkin because I thought he will give this incredible tale a feeling of documentary reality. And I can trust him; he's honest. He must have known he was blowing the *Gunn* job. He's honest and I wanted an honest man."

In the intervening years, Blatty had also been in touch with

Friedkin over the possibility of his directing another Blatty script, an adaptation of his 1966 novel *Twinkle, Twinkle, 'Killer' Kane*, the author's first examination of the nature of faith (later filmed as *The Ninth Configuration*). Both men were interested in working on the project; the studios were not.

And Warners were still not very interested in Friedkin. They had drawn up a list of potential directors that included Stanley Kubrick, Arthur Penn and Mike Nichols, amongst others. Penn was committed to teaching at Yale for the coming year, Kubrick wanted to produce himself (and inevitably film in England, the adopted homeland he now refused to leave) and Nichols, coming off the flop of *Catch-22*, had serious doubts about laying the whole success of the picture on the shoulders of a twelve-year-old girl.

"But they refused to put Friedkin on this list," Blatty explains. "And then I discovered that they were negotiating with another director [Mark Rydell] and I went mad, and I threatened a law suit. In the meantime I'd seen *The French Connection*, which redoubled my passion for getting Friedkin. And they hadn't seen it, but they at least agreed to look at it. And they did and they wound up hiring Friedkin. Had I the technical expertise to be a director at that time, I would have asked to direct it. But I was terrified. Every great director on our list was terrified. Only Billy wasn't."

After much re-reading, Friedkin was still immensely impressed with the novel. "It has a beginning, a middle and an end," he says. "How many works of contemporary fiction since then can you say that about? Most of this stuff that other guys have written, thinking they're working in Blatty's genre, is garbage. Let's say that you want to refer to *The Exorcist* novel as a horror novel. Well, you've got Stephen King who writes sort of lame pastiches in my opinion, and you've got Dean Koontz whose work is garbage. *The Exorcist* is a literate and profound story that is not just trading in on jolts and shakes, and such. It's not trying to scare you, it's trying to move you. And it succeeds in moving its reader while holding them totally. I'm not a fan of that type of literature if it is typified by, let's say, Koontz and King. Although King is better, I can't even put the two of them in the same category.

"Stephen King is very often readable and sometimes very good; Blatty's novel is great. It's a great novel. It's a great story. In the seventies of course, we were interested in stories first. Now they're not. Now the only kind of movies that get made really are ones that promise a whole bunch of explosions and stuff. The story is meaningless. The characters are just there to trigger explosions. But in the seventies, the story was important and *The Exorcist* was a great story. A lot of people who were involved with movies at that time couldn't see it, but it was a great story."

It appears that one of the people who couldn't see it was Blatty himself. "He didn't do the novel," Friedkin offers simply when discussing Blatty's first crack at turning his novel into a screenplay. "He left out the Iraq prologue; he had a whole bunch of horror film effects written in – zooms and weird angles. He had a sequence that can only be described as a compendium of horror schlock effects, references to Hitler and Stalin, and other catastrophic events and people through history. Then he reduced a lot of the scenes to shrill one or two liners, rather than letting the scenes play out. I thought the script was frankly terrible and I told Bill that."

"I was very conscious of the fact that only a limited amount of material could be presented," counters Blatty. "I didn't want to give up anything; I didn't want to give up the Karl subplot. I didn't want to give up the theological discussions; I didn't want to give up anything. I felt well, I have to give something up, what am I gonna do? So I said 'I'll compress the early part of the book, and the way to compress it is to use flashbacks and a very stylistic approach.' And even with that the script ran almost 200 pages. Billy didn't want me to do it that way; he thought I was not being faithful to the novel.'

"By this time he knew how much I loved the novel," continues Friedkin. "And I said 'I really want to shoot this novel.' And I marked up my copy of the book and I said 'I want this dialogue, this scene. The only thing I want to do is put it all in consecutive order. No flashbacks, no jumping around the way you're able to do in the novel, no referencing back to what had happened before with this person or whatever. Just start here, interact and move onto the final scene where they leave the house.' So I marked up the book and whenever I saw him varying from the dialogue or the scene structure, I sort of jumped on him and went back to the novel and said 'Bill, it's all here. We don't really need to write a screenplay, the book is a script; we need to edit it. That's all we really need to do. We'll edit the novel and that's the screenplay.' And after months of this he got the idea and he was doing it. There had to be some adjustment of course, from the page to the screen. But basically it's an extremely faithful adaptation of the book. The dream sequence I sort of invented in a way. And once I got to Iraq, I improvised certain things that I saw there and put those in the scenes. But the scenes throughout were extremely faithful to that novel, which I still think is a great novel."

"There was my first draft," says Blatty. "Then I did one with Billy. So there were only two. I would change pages and things happened on set, but there were just two major drafts."

By now the book was a bestseller and all eyes at Warner Brothers were on the production. Despite the controversial nature of the novel, the company remained surprisingly supportive, at no time pressurising Blatty to drop any of the book's more extreme moments or language. "Even in the crucifix masturbation scene," Blatty says today, still with some amazement, "it was indicated very specifically that it really was not to be graphic. You wouldn't see too much. We observed it pretty faithfully, but I must say when I looked at the scene it shocked the hell out of me. I wanted to look away and I still do. But no, I never heard a word out of Warners."

"They were reluctant brides at the time," adds Friedkin. "I had to drag them to the altar on every decision but, ultimately they gave way because they didn't know anything either and I had just won an Academy Award by then, so they figured I must know something that they didn't know. They had no idea how this film could ever be pulled off or if they could ever release it. But they did sort of indulge it, reluctantly, every step of the way while trying to frustrate it from time to time as well."

Blatty's primary concern for the film was to get the backing and support of the Church. The book had been well received by the Church as a whole, with Blatty garnering some of his best notices in religious publications such as the Vatican literary journal, *Civilta Cattolica*. The production received the blessing of three Catholic priests, some of whom appeared both on screen and worked as technical advisors off-camera. Father Thomas Bermingham, Blatty's former tutor, who would take on the role of the President of Georgetown University was one of them. He had subsequently risen to become the vice-provinsal of the Jesuit's New York Province, based at Fordham University in the Bronx.

Father John Nicola was brought on board as the film's chief technical consultant on all matters relating to the Church. Nicola was the assistant director at the National Shrine of the Immaculate Conception and was one of the Church's leading authorities on demonology and possession, a subject he had studied for over two decades when the film company came knocking at his church door.

The third, and most visible of the film's Catholic guardians, was Father William O'Malley, who had come to the production via a circuitous route. Based at McQuaid High School in Rochester at the time of the novel's publication, O'Malley was asked by the Rochester Public Library to review Blatty's work, a task he initially balked at. When eventually written, O'Malley's review totalled nine pages and praised Blatty's tale for his theological stance, even if the reviewer was more unsure of the language used by Chris MacNeil than her daughter. Knowing Blatty's background, the priest sent him a copy of the review and was pleasantly surprised to receive a lengthy reply from the author.

Blatty and his wife were due to travel to New York and arranged to have dinner with both Father Bermingham and Father O'Malley. O'Malley and Blatty hit it off and talked long into the night, the author turned producer now convinced that he had found the right man to play the role of Father Dyer. O'Malley, who had in his pre-collared days studied at the Royal Academy of Dramatic Art in London and had, ever since, been a staple of whatever theatre his community had to offer, leapt at the chance and agreed to meet Friedkin to finalise the offer. In typical confrontational style, Friedkin agreed to meet O'Malley at the same time as he was giving an interview to *Screw* magazine. Unphased by this, Bill O'Malley chimed in with his views on the novel and opened up a debate on celibacy that, presumably, left the *Screw* hack reeling. It was enough to convince Friedkin.

The Jewish-raised Friedkin took as his first task, the opportunity to immerse himself in the ways of the Catholic faith. He began by attending mass up to five times a week. "I was not born a Catholic or raised a Catholic. I knew nothing really about the tenets of the Church. I started to do a lot of reading. I spoke to Jesuit priests, some of whom became involved with the film as actors and technical advisers. I went to mass very often, and in the reading I did about the church and in my experience of the mass and the Eucharist, and what I consider to be the profound tenets of the church, my growing realisation was that all the great art, all the great painting, which will never ever in my opinion be duplicated, was done in the name of the Catholic church. And most of it in celebration of the infant Jesus. And it opened for me a lot of the profound mysteries and beauty that is embodied in the Church."

Friedkin was so consumed by the discoveries he was making that he seriously considered converting to Catholicism. "But ultimately I thought this church, like all other organised religions, is driven by men and not Gods. And that while some of the ideas were great, a lot of it was no more, no less, than an exclusive club with a lot of man-made rules, some of which made no particular sense to me. Nevertheless, I did immerse myself in the religion and I found in it what I think I needed to be able to make that film respectfully."

"At the time I didn't think Friedkin's religious background was important," recalls Blatty, "but looking back on it, it was a very fortunate thing. I don't know what Billy's beliefs were or are, but I know he's from a Jewish background and, in retrospect, I think you either have to be a Catholic or a Jew to correctly interpret this material – to have the proper sensitivity and sensibility. I think, for example, of John Boorman and *Exorcist II*. Utterly the wrong man, he never got it."

Bringing his documentarian approach to the material, Friedkin was adamant that the medical scenes in the movie, where Chris MacNeil searches ultimately in vain for a logical, scientific explanation for her daughter Regan's illness, be as realistic as possible and he spent an equal amount of time researching the latest medical routines.

"I became aware that since Blatty had written the novel, medical science had made tremendous progress and that some of the events in the book were not current with brain examinations at that time. And I went to the NYU medical centre, the radiological department. And I saw what they were doing now in medical examinations of the brain – the arteriogram, for example. And it was fascinating for me and it was the state-of-the-art then. Now, of course, the state-of-the-art is MRI. Then the arteriogram was the ultimate test of brain damage and I was allowed to see one taking place from a control room. So I persuaded Bill that, rather than memorialise what had occurred in examination of the brain, we should go with what they were doing at the time of the film. So that was another element that I brought into the story that wasn't in the book. And when I showed Bill this stuff he was equally impressed and said 'Yeah, let's have that.'"

One thing Friedkin could not have allowed for during the pre-production of *The Exorcist* was that he would accidentally bump into the cousin of the boy from the original 1949 Mount Rainier incident. Friedkin had hired a house on Fire Island for the duration of production. His next-door neighbour introduced him to a friend, an American Airlines pilot, who told Friedkin how the novel had reminded him of some long forgotten events in his own family history. Intrigued, Friedkin (who by now had discovered the name of the family involved) mentioned the name of the original boy's father. He was the pilot's uncle; the possessed boy had been his cousin. The pilot put Friedkin in touch with his aunt, who clearly remembered the events. She spoke to Friedkin for over an hour, all off the record.

Taking this as a good omen for the production, Friedkin incorporated many of the details the aunt related into Blatty's script.

For his crew, Friedkin retained the services of two of his allies from *The French Connection*. Chris Newman would once again handle the sound, whilst Owen Roizman signed on as director of photography. "When I went back to New York to do *The French Connection*, I didn't really have a lot of respect for the New York cameramen who were prevalent then. So I went to see a friend of mine, a man named Dick Dibono, who was the owner of General Cameras, where we always used to rent our equipment. Dick was a really good guy and I said 'Dick, are they any good young cameramen around?' And he said 'Yeah, there's one guy who I think is very good, who I think you'll like. He said his name is Owen Roizman and he's only done a couple of commercials, but I think the guy's really good and if you want to go with someone new, he's the guy.' He said 'I can get his reel for you.' And I said 'I really don't want to look at a reel of commercials. But I'll meet him.' Dick had this kitchen in his building and he was a very good cook of Italian food – wonderful – and he made a lunch for Owen and myself and himself, and I met Owen and I thought he was a nice enough guy and I told him how I saw the film, what I was planning on doing with it, the way I wanted to do it. He said 'That sounds great to me' and I said 'OK, you're hired.' 'Cause I liked him. A lot of people can't imagine I'd never seen anything of his. But the equivalent of Dick Dibono's endorsement was enough to me."

With Friedkin's key technical people in place, the next step was casting.

MAX VON SYDOW

In casting *The Exorcist*, there was only one character that Blatty and
Friedkin instantly, and unequivocally, agreed on. Blatty had based
Lancaster Merrin's character on the life and workings of the
theologian Theilard de Chardin, but visually he took as his
inspiration a man named Gerald Lancaster Harding, an antiquities
curator Blatty had known in Palestine, who was instrumental in
discovering the Dead Sea Scrolls. Blatty showed a picture of Harding
– whose middle name had also lent itself to Merrin – and Friedkin had
an instantaneous response. "Max von Sydow I wanted immediately. I
had no other choice. Blatty had told me he'd based the character of
Father Merrin on Theilard de Chardin, the French Catholic priest,
missionary, archaeologist. We went to von Sydow and offered him
the role. He was then in his late thirties, I believe [he was, in fact,
forty-three], so he required a lot of make-up to adequately or
accurately portray Merrin. But we wanted him and went after him
right away."

Max von Sydow was born Carl Adolf von Sydow in Lund, Sweden,
on 10 April 1929. A shy child, he would listen avidly to the folk tales
and fairy stories his father, a university professor of comparative
folklore, would recount. When he was in high school, a lavish
municipal theatre opened in the town nearby. It was von Sydow's
first experience of theatre and it prompted him and some friends to

form their own amateur theatrical company, performing a number of Swedish plays, by the likes of Strindberg and Jalmar Bergman. On deciding to become a professional actor, von Sydow trained at the Stockholm Royal Dramatic Theatre School, rapidly establishing himself as a force to be reckoned with in Swedish theatre, transferring to movies, at the age of twenty, with 1949's *Only A Mother*. On film, von Sydow made his mark through a string of associations with Ingmar Bergman, such seminal works as *Wild Strawberries*, *Through A Glass Darkly* and, perhaps most famously, as Death's chess playing challenger in *The Seventh Seal*.

As Bergman's movies began to win an audience among the arthouses and college campuses of America in the late fifties and early sixties, von Sydow soon found his unique presence was in demand Stateside. He began at the top as it were, playing Jesus Christ in George Stevens' lengthy, all-star epic *The Greatest Story Ever Told*, before falling into the trap of essaying various generic Cold War warriors with matching macs in such forgettable capers as *The Kremlin Letter* and *The Quiller Memorandum*.

Given his wealthy European background, *The Exorcist* held an instant appeal for von Sydow. "To me, the Devil has never been scary," he insists. "I was brought up with Scandinavian fairy tales and folk tales, and in many of those, the Devil is kind of ridiculous. He is always a loser."

Max von Sydow: Filmography Pre-*Exorcist*

Only A Mother (1949)
Miss Julie (1951)
No Man's Woman (1953)
The Seventh Seal (1957)
Wild Strawberries (1957)
Brink Of Life (1958)
The Magician (1958)
The Virgin Spring (1960)
Through A Glass Darkly (1961)
The Swedish Mistress (1962)
Winter Light (1963)
The Greatest Story Ever Told (1965)
The Reward (1965)
Hawaii (1966)
The Quiller Memorandum (1966)
Here Is Your Life (1966)
Hour Of The Wolf (1968)
The Shame (1968)
Made In Sweden (1969)
A Passion (1969)
The Kremlin Letter (1970)
The Emigrant (1971)
The Touch (1971)
The Night Visitor (1971)
Embassy (1972)
The New Land (1973)
The Exorcist (1973)

ELLEN BURSTYN

Shirley MacLaine, despite being the inspiration for the character of Chris MacNeil in Blatty's novel, was out of the running for the film role, having opted for the similarly-themed *Possession Of Joel Delaney*. This left the role of Chris both wide open and one of the most sought-after female leads in recent Hollywood history. Once again, the studio drew up a short list consisting of Audrey Hepburn, Jane Fonda and Anne Bancroft.

"I had always felt that Chris should be, if not played by an unknown," says Friedkin, "then someone fresh, someone who was not associated with a lot of movie history. But there was nothing I could do about the fact, if they could get one of those three women. I wasn't going to piss on it because they were certainly three of the best actresses in the world."

Top of the wish list was Audrey Hepburn, who agreed to do the role if they would film in Rome, where she was now married and settled. Given the vast technical difficulties Friedkin predicted for the movie, and the importance of Georgetown as a location (not to mention the fact that all the characters, and the crew hired to date, were American), this quickly meant that Hepburn was out of the frame.

Anne Bancroft was also eager to do the role but fell pregnant at the time. Friedkin states that she went as far as to suggest that the

picture be postponed until after she'd given birth, a definite no go with Warners. This left Jane Fonda, who turned the movie down in no uncertain terms. Says Friedkin: "She was in her anti-Vietnam phase, anti-American phase, anti-American life phase and she made a comment to the effect of why would I want to be associated with this piece of capitalist horseshit? So she went the way of all flesh." (Blatty actually quotes Fonda as sending the message "Why would any studio want to make this capitalist rip-off bullshit?", a statement the actress later told the author she never made, opting to pass on the movie simply because, as she put it, "I don't believe in magic.")

Through his dealings with Peter Bogdanovich, Friedkin had noticed Ellen Burstyn in her Oscar-nominated role in Bogdanovich's *The Last Picture Show*. Even so, he was surprised when she called his office at Warner Brothers and insisted that the role of Chris MacNeil was meant for her. "She had never had any lead roles, but I thought she was interesting. When she called me, she seemed very intelligent on the phone and said 'Will you at least meet me for this part?' And I said 'Alright, when can you come in?' And she said 'I'd rather not come into your office, that's sort of formal and embarrassing.' So she asked where I lived and I told her, and she said 'Look I'm on your way home, why don't you drive up to my house?' So I did one day. It was a kind of hippie pad in the Hollywood hills. And she was wearing a big shift. She was very heavy-set. She was probably about fifty pounds heavier than you see in the film, and one of the first things she did was offer me some grass, which I don't smoke, have never been interested in and was sort of turned-off by. But then she started to talk and tell me about her spiritual and religious beliefs. And I was very impressed with her and her knowledge of the book, and I told her at that time that these other actresses were under consideration and that the studio really wanted a star. And she said 'Well, I believe that it's fate that I will do this part.' I said 'Good luck to you.' And I left, never thinking that I would have to use her.'

As Hepburn, Bancroft and Fonda all bailed out, Friedkin maintained a phone-dialogue with Burstyn. Eventually, he went to

Ted Ashley, head of Warners and suggested the actress for the role. After all, by now she had her Academy Award nomination, so Friedkin wasn't exactly playing a wild card. "I remember Ashley's exact words were 'Bill, you know I have complete faith in you, and I know you'll do a great job with this picture, but Ellen Burstyn will play this part over my dead body. Do you understand what I'm saying? Over my dead body!!!' Then he started to sing it and he got carried away in explaining to me the significance of the image of his dead body and my stepping over it to hand this role to Ellen Burstyn. It didn't look too good." Friedkin eventually did a screen test with Burstyn, which, with every one else out of the running, convinced Ashley that she was right for the role, without his needing to die or, indeed, be stepped over.

Burstyn remembers her casting somewhat differently to Friedkin: "We met and we talked and he told me 'I'm not gonna keep you dangling, it's between you and . . .' and he mentioned another actress. And he said 'I'm flying to New York to see her tomorrow and I'll let you know right away whether it's you or her.' And I thought that was wonderful of him not to keep me dangling.

"The next morning he called me from New York and said 'Alright, you've got the part,'" Burstyn recalled for the BBC. "And I said 'Oh, you saw her?' And he said 'No, I ran into her in the deli last night and she looked like hell.' And I said 'Well, Billy that's not fair. I look like hell in the deli too.' And he said 'Well, that's the way the cookie crumbles, what can I tell you?' So that's how I got the part."

Burstyn intuitively responded to the character of Chris MacNeil. "I thought of her as a tap dancer. Long after that I think, during the course of the movie, Bill Blatty told me that he had based the character on his friend Shirley MacLaine, who in fact, had been a dancer and who had come to Hollywood through Broadway musicals, which I didn't know. So there must have been something in his writing that told me that." Burstyn's research – which included her writing a history for the character of Chris MacNeil – led her to examine the scientific research done on the 1949 case.

Ellen Burstyn, real name Edna Rae Gillooly, first saw the light of day on 7 December 1932 in Detroit. With a seemingly callous disregard for her original (or indeed many subsequent) moniker, she headed for New York and then Texas at the age of eighteen, to make it as a model named Edna Rae. Shortly afterwards, her friends and business associates knew her as Keri Flynn, the Montreal-based night-club chorus line dancer. It was one Erica Dean who landed a Hollywood screen test in the mid-fifties, but it was Ellen MacRae who made her Broadway debut in *Fair Game* in 1957. She stuck with this name for most of the sixties, including her stint on the popular television show *The Doctors*. Her name was changed for one final time to Ellen Burstyn when she married at the tail end of that decade.

A stint studying the 'method' with Lee Strasberg in New York saw Burstyn reinvent herself as a powerfully accomplished actress, landing a Best Supporting Actress Oscar nomination for 1971's *The Last Picture Show*, and winning critical plaudits opposite Jack Nicholson and Bruce Dern in Bob Rafelson's *The King of Marvin Gardens*.

Ellen Burstyn: Filmography Pre-*Exorcist*

For Those Who Think Young (1964)
Goodbye Charlie (1964)
Tropic Of Cancer (1970)
Alex In Wonderland (1970)
The Last Picture Show (1971)
The King of Marvin Gardens (1972)
The Exorcist (1973)

JASON MILLER

"**B**illy ran like the wind from star names," recalls Blatty. "I proposed Marlon Brando to play Karras and Billy just hated that idea. Not because Brando wouldn't have been wonderful in the part, but because it would've been a Marlon Brando movie, and so on down the line. I think Gene Hackman wanted to play Karras, but Billy was very happy to have a relatively unknown cast. The title was the star."

Brando and Hackman weren't the only names being mooted for the plum role of Father Damien Karras. Jack Nicholson and Paul Newman were also in the running, but Friedkin was holding out for someone new, someone unexpected and, more importantly, someone who could become the role of the faith-troubled priest, an actor who wouldn't bring the baggage of a movie star to the screen. He thought he'd found all that in Stacy Keach, then an up-and-coming young actor who was making a name for himself on stage: "I didn't really see him in the role, but I had nobody else, so we signed him."

Shortly before Keach put pen to paper, Friedkin saw a performance of a play called *That Championship Season* in New York. It was written by a young actor/playwright named Jason Miller. "I liked the play," Friedkin remarks. "I thought it was very well written. But more than that, it seemed to have an aura of failed Catholicism running right through it. It was obviously written by someone who understood the way Catholic boys become Catholic men and turn away from the Church. It had a deep understanding of people who were raised in a very strict way in the faith, and then abandoned it but it never left them. This is one of the things I perceived from the play."

Jason Miller was born, the only child of an Irish Catholic family, in Scranton, Pennsylvania on 22 April 1939. Miller's play *The Winner* won him a regional playwriting award whilst he was still in high school in Scranton. His mother was a retired teacher of mentally handicapped children and her family background of Pennsylvanian miners became the inspiration for Miller's first professionally produced play *Nobody Hears A Broken Drum*.

Friedkin quizzed Juliet Taylor, his New York casting director, about the playwright. She knew Miller vaguely as a bit part actor. Friedkin recalls that, "he was at this time working on a milk delivery truck in Flushing, New York." For reasons he still can't quite fathom, Friedkin had Taylor set up a meeting with Miller: "We had a very inconsequential meeting. He didn't know why the hell he was there. I must say I didn't know why he was there either. I was not especially looking for an actor. I didn't know what he looked like. But I was interested in his play and wanted to talk to him about it. He came into the room and I guess we spent about an hour together. And it was difficult for both of us. It was uncommunicative. I guess he thought maybe I was interested in buying the play to make a film out of it. I asked him if he had read *The Exorcist*, and he hadn't. But he told me that he had, in fact, studied for the priesthood with the Jesuits. He had spent three years in a Jesuit school and had had a crisis of faith and had to drop out. And I thought he's a very interesting guy, but I went back to California and signed Stacy Keach to play the part."

A few days later, however, Friedkin was surprised to find the uncommunicative playwright on the phone. "He said 'Hey, I read that book you were talking about, and I think it's really terrific, and I really think that I could play that part.' I said 'What part?' And he said 'Father Karras.' I said 'We've already signed an actor to do it.' He said 'You're making a mistake, you're making a big mistake. I am that guy.

Jason Miller

Will you at least shoot a screen test with me?' I said 'Why? I've got another actor for this role. What's the point?' I don't know why I did it, but I went to the Warners people and I said 'I'm gonna fly this guy out and shoot a screen test with him.' And they had never heard of him and they said 'Are you crazy?' and I said 'Probably.' "

Friedkin offered to fly Miller out the next day but the actor, who was afraid of flying, told the director that he would take a train and be there in a week. When Miller eventually turned up, Friedkin set up a test on an empty stage, with Ellen Burstyn.

"I put a camera over Ellen's shoulder and had her interview him, just had him talk about himself – his life, what he had done, his feelings about life, his feelings about his work, and all that. And then I had them improvise one of the scenes from the film, the scene where Chris MacNeil tells Father Karras that she thinks her daughter is possessed. I had them do a long walk on an empty soundstage and improvise this scene. Then I had Jason just say the mass in an extreme close-up. And I told him I wanted him to say mass as if he really believed every word, not the way most priests do it today, where they just rattle it out. We did it and after the test Ellen came to me and said 'What did you do that for? You're not going to use him?' And I said 'Why?' And she said 'Because he can't act. He's not an actor. Also he's short, he's shorter than I am and my vision of Father Karras is I have to look up to him; I have to collapse in his arms, he's got to be a heroic figure.'

"The next day I saw the rushes and I thought they were great. Something happened between Jason's face and the camera that I couldn't even really see when I was filming it, but there it was. The evidence was there. And I looked at it and I said 'That's the guy.' "

Warners (and Blatty) were less sold on the idea. "Bill Blatty didn't want him, Burstyn didn't want him, nobody wanted him, which made me want him even more I suppose. And I got Warners to pay off Stacy Keach, which was a difficult thing to do. They had to pay him in full. And we hired Jason. And at that moment I threw all caution to the wind in the making of this film and I guess I was unconsciously relying on the Movie Gods to give me ballast. I was out with a leap into the void."

When speaking to journalist Mark Kermode, Miller remembered events slightly differently: "My agent said this guy Bill Friedkin wants to talk to you; he's gonna do *The Exorcist*. I said 'Well, they want me to do the screenplay or what?' My agent said 'No, he saw the play and he's very, very laudatory about your work. He just wants to meet you.' So I went up to the hotel room and there's Friedkin. I'd never met him before. I said 'Hi, how are you? How do you do? What are we here for? You want me to do the screenplay right?' He said 'No.' I said 'Well, what do you want me to do?' And he said 'I want you to do a screen-test for Father Karras'. I said 'You what? I've never acted in a movie in my life. I'm a playwright.' He said 'That's alright. I looked, I saw your picture, I gotta hunch.' And *The Exorcist* was full of hunches, so I said 'OK.' "

Jason Miller's play *That Championship Season* was awarded the New York Drama Critics' Best Play Award in 1972, and a Tony Award the following year, the same year that Miller received the Pulitzer Prize for Drama. He made his movie debut in *The Exorcist*.

Before filming began, Miller spent three weeks living with the Jesuits in Georgetown. (Ironically, whilst attending the University of Scranton, he had heard the story of the 1949 case: "The same priest, the same Jesuit, told Blatty the story when he got to Georgetown. When he came to the University of Scranton he told us the same story.") The Jesuits showed him where they stored the clothing of dead Jesuit priests – a vast cellar full of black suits, coats and priestly paraphernalia. It was from this collection that Miller chose the wardrobe that he would wear in the film.

"Most of them liked the book very much," Miller said of the Jesuits at the time, "But most of them think they're Karras, anyway. The character in the book is in his forties and I'm in my thirties. The age difference may bother people. Apparently, all priests feel a questioning of faith in their forties. It's called the male menopause. But one of the dangers is that their training leads them to a kind of mental pitfall and they become terribly over-analytical, ringing out the juice from things to find a kind of sterile logic. . . . The Jesuits encourage free thinking amongst themselves because they realise that suppression is the first way to destroy themselves. They're really a unique, special, and terrifying order of men."

It was whilst staying with the Jesuits however, that Miller became privy to a vital piece of research – Father Bowdern's original diary from the 1949 Maryland case. "Blatty did not see this diary," Miller explained to journalist Peter Travers. "I had to get it from the chancellery office in Washington DC. This priest kept a diary for two months. It was scratched out in places and words were changed, but it tells how the boy spoke in three different languages, and how there was movement of furniture. There was also a description from the boy of what hell was, in very graphic, Old Testament terms. According to the diary, there was constant urination. They had to keep changing the bed sheets. The boy was fourteen years old, and spoke in Latin and French. At one point, he broke the nose of another Jesuit priest in attendance. That diary is the truest description of possession I have ever read, next to Blatty's book."

CHAPTER NINE

LINDA BLAIR

The key to the success of *The Exorcist* was always going to be the girl. Friedkin, Blatty and everyone involved with the project all knew that finding the right twelve-year-old to play Regan MacNeil was crucial; Mike Nichols had been so convinced of this that he passed on the project for that very reason. Juliet Taylor in New York and Nessa Hyams at Warner in LA had seen over 500 girls.

"There were no twelve-year-old girls you were gonna find," says Friedkin. "At one point we gave up on the idea of a twelve-year-old girl and I was looking at sixteen-year-old girls who looked younger. I never thought we'd ever come up with a twelve- or thirteen-year-old to do this, but we did." (At one point, Blatty had jokingly suggested they look for a "twenty-five-year-old midget.")

Twelve-year-old child catalogue model Linda Blair had seen several girls from her modelling agency go up for the role of Regan. But the agency opted not to send Blair, whose acting experience to date was confined to walk-on roles in instantly forgotten movies. Her mother wasn't happy about the agency's lack of faith in her talented offspring and took her along to Taylor herself.

"I had done two small movies when I was ten," recalls Blair, "A soap opera and, when I was about twelve, my ambition was to be a veterinarian. And I told my mother 'I don't really want do this anymore.' Modelling was harder than it looks. And we were driving home, we were right next to the UN, and mother said to me 'We have an interview for a movie.' And a movie is ever so exciting. I didn't grow up in Hollywood so it was great. We knew the title – *The Exorcist*. It didn't mean anything to either of us."

The 500 or so candidates were whittled down to a list of twelve, Blair included. "I went in and met with Juliet Taylor who was casting the picture," Blair explained to journalist Kermode. "And they gave me this dialogue which was like a paragraph of the worst language you could ever imagine. But I was always told to be professional – do what you do, do what you're told to do, and so I went in and read this filth, and when I was done I went downstairs and, like, how am I gonna tell my mom about this? She was always very good about not pushing me, so she said 'How'd it go?' I said 'Fine.' "

The chosen dozen girls met with Friedkin, who had them all read two key scenes – the moment when Chris first asks her daughter about the Ouija board and learns of Captain Howdy, and the bed scene where we first see Regan in the grip of the demon. After the various readings, six of these girls were asked to do a proper run-through of the scenes.

"They liked Linda in New York and so I then met with Linda and I knew immediately that she was the one," Friedkin recalls. "I met with her and she was very bright and personable. Her mother was very charming and sweet; she sat in the room. I met with several other young women too and it was impossible. You couldn't even reach them on this level. I said to Linda 'Do you know anything about *The Exorcist*?' And she said 'Oh yeah, it's about a little girl who gets possessed by a devil and she does a whole lot of bad things.' I said 'What sort of things?' She said 'Well, she hits her mother across the face, pushes a man out her window and she masturbates with a crucifix.' Linda was twelve, I guess, at the time. And I said 'Do you know what that means – what you just said – masturbate?' She said, 'Yeah, it's like jerking off, isn't it?' And I said 'Yes, it is. Have you ever done that?' And she said 'Sure. Haven't you?' And I turned to her mother and I said 'I'd like to test her.' So I shot a test with her and Ellen, and it was clear this was the girl."

Linda Blair

(Blair herself denies ever having said the above: "The truth is he asked me what I thought of the book, what mother thought of it. And I just asked mom like 'I don't understand. How do they make a little girl jump up and down on the bed? How does the head spin round? It's the same questions that the audience ask me to this day." And in Peter Travers and Stephanie Reiff's book *The Story Behind The Exorcist*, Friedkin himself attributes these remarks to a nine-year-old he also auditioned.)

Friedkin did a series of tests with Blair. "Billy met with me probably six more times, just talking" Blair continued. " Which I am very grateful for, and anybody should be, because what he was doing was he wanted to see how stable I was. And of course, growing up in Connecticut, raised around dogs, cats, horses, land, nature, I grew up a country girl. So he realised I was very stable, went to public school. I'm a Christian, and in my religion we never discussed the Devil, so to me it was a fictitious character, like people think of Frankenstein. Then he would have meetings where he'd ask me to start acting out things. He'd say 'Now, what I want you to do is get on the couch and writhe around in pain.' Well, I was just embarrassed. But I commend him that he made sure I was stable."

Ellen Burstyn was not impressed with Linda's test, but Friedkin had kept the cameras running on the two of them after they'd finished the scene. It was Blair's naturalness with the actress, when she was unaware of the pressures of performing for the camera, that ultimately convinced Friedkin he had found his Regan.

"When Warner Brothers finally did pick me," continued the actress "It was like three months of testing. We did make-up tests and, of course, little girls don't want to be this ugly creature. It wasn't like it was any fun. But it was a big movie."

Linda Blair was born 22 January 1959 in St Louis, Missouri. Her family relocated to Westport, Connecticut when she was two years old. She started modelling at the age of nine in nearby New York. A keen young horse rider, who regularly showed her pony in competition (for Christmas, Friedkin, Blatty and Warners presented her with a gelding that she promptly named 'Best Director' in honour of Billy's Academy Award), Blair's catalogue modelling led to small roles in movies and on television.

Linda Blair: Filmography Pre-*Exorcist*

The Way We Live Now (1970)
The Sporting Club (1971)
The Exorcist (1973)

Friedkin fleshed out his cast with Kitty Winn as Sharon Spencer, Chris MacNeil's assistant, and Jack MacGowran as film director Burke Dennings. MacGowran was a last-minute replacement for real life director J. Lee Thompson, who had helmed one of Blatty's early movies, *John Goldfarb, Please Come Home*, and signed earlier to the project. (There was some speculation as to whether or not Blatty had modelled the director in the novel on any of his former associates.)

Of all the characters, Blatty probably felt closest to Lt William Kinderman. They shared a Christian name and many saw the wily, world-weary detective as an alter-ego for the writer. Sadly, for Blatty, many of the character's idiosyncrasies and his general approach in the novel, were absent from the screenplay. This was in part due to the fact that in 1971 Peter Falk had debuted on American television in the role of Lt Columbo, a detective whose working methods very much echoed Kinderman's 'mind-like-a-steel-trap-masked-by-phoney-bumbling' nature.

Friedkin was watching a play in California when he was struck by a balding, middle-aged, moustachioed actor and thought, this is Kinderman. He failed to notice at the time that this actor was, in fact, Lee J. Cobb minus his usual toupee. "Lee J. Cobb was one of the three or four greatest actors in America since the thirties. Blatty had some other ideas which I thought were stupid and ludicrous – they were friends of his."

With the parts of Fathers Bermingham and O'Malley already set, the cast of *The Exorcist* was ready, quite literally, for 'action'. "It was a combination of first choices, complete unknowns, people who had never been in a movie before, and an actress in the lead who had never done a lead in a film before," says Friedkin, when considering his casting choices. "And I must say, the only thing I had any real confidence in was my own ability to bring the thing off. I had this thing somewhere on the tip of my tongue or in the back of my mind, or in my back pocket somewhere, and I knew I could pull it off. Without any real reason to think so, because as I speak of these decisions now they seem to be insane. At the time they seemed perfectly logical to me, even though they were extremely unorthodox. I could have had any star I wanted.

"I think if I made one single great contribution to it, it's holding out for the cast that I did, and going for the cast that I did, each of whom are now inseparable from those roles."

CHAPTER·
TEN

BAD HAIR DAYS

Any of the technical problems inherent in bringing *The Exorcist* to the screen would not be solved until well into filming – a trial-and-error process that, in part, accounted for the film's lengthy shooting schedule of nine months. One thing that had to be finalised, however, before the cameras could start turning, was the look of the demonic Regan. Make-up expert Dick Smith was charged with the task.

"I met with Billy," recalls the make-up legend. "And I heard this tape that Billy had of the exorcism of the little boy that the book was based on. And it was kind of impressive, with howling and mooing sounds and things like that. Obviously, something like this could be faked so you take it with a pinch of salt. All I was concerned about at this point was not whether an exorcism had taken place or was even theoretically possible, I was just dealing with the problems of the movie."

By the time he joined the crew of *The Exorcist*, Smith was already Hollywood's leading make-up expert. Having founded the first make-up department in television at NBC in the fifties, he had gone on to age Marlon Brando for *The Godfather*, and turn Dustin Hoffman into a 121-year-old man in *Little Big Man*.

Smith began his task by trawling through all the books he could discover on demonology, closely examining any drawings he could find of demons and devils. The next stage was to make a number of life masks of Blair. "Linda was brought in for me to meet and look over," Smith recalls, "And, oh my God, here's this sweet little twelve-year-old girl with apple cheeks and a butter-ball nose, a lovely sweet face. And to make her into a monster was quite challenging."

From this meeting he produced around a half dozen plaster busts of Linda's head and then used modelling clay to build a number of designs on to them. Smith designed several different make-ups before consulting with Friedkin and narrowing it down to the ones they thought would work best.

"Billy gave me a kind of free hand. He wasn't even there in New York when this started. In any case, I was provided with a cameraman and an operator and an assistant to run some screen tests. So within a few days I did five different concepts, which were all quite different. The first one I did was truly witch-like and overboard. I did both Linda and Eileen Dietz (her double) to see also whether I could make them look alike. Well, this extreme thing with wild black hair and bushy eyebrows did at least make her look evil and witchy and all that, and did kind of disguise her face, but was obviously way overboard. Some of the other concepts were very moderate – just kind of ugly, nasty little girls. Then there was one that was somewhere in between. And this seemed to have possibilities. Billy saw these tests and he decided he would go for the style that I showed in the final test, so I then went ahead and developed that further."

Regan's make-up needed to evolve over the course of the film as her possession becomes more apparent. Smith ultimately designed four stages for this. The first stage was simple fresh cuts that appeared on Regan's face and body (their on-screen appearance was, at times, achieved by a gossamer-thin piece of latex being pulled off the relative area by well-hidden fishing wire). Then the second stage involved the use of latex appliances, altering the shape of Blair's face and brow, and offering deeper, more repugnant pus-oozing cuts. The third stage was a more distorted, extreme version of this, whilst the fourth and final stage, during the final exorcism, went the other way and was, at Friedkin's suggestion, a less severe form of

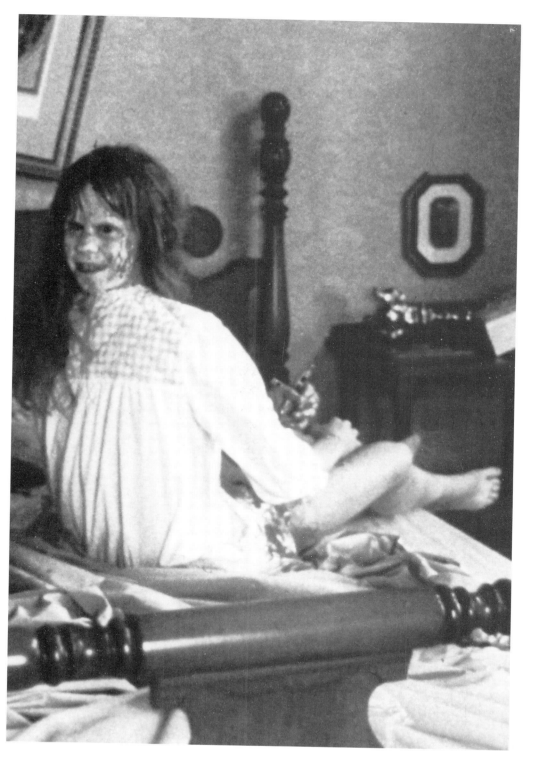

the demonic extreme – a chance to once again see the girl inside.

Blair's make-up needed approximately two hours to apply. The twelve-year-old actress accepted being transfigured into a demon very well, although she was less pleased about the liquid wax that had to be applied to her hair and took at least three washes to rinse out. In the end, Smith simply used shampoo on her hair to achieve the same effect.

Blair's make-up was so elaborate and time-consuming for its day that one studio executive at Warner Brothers asked why she couldn't put it on herself at home in the morning and then drive to work on time, already made-up.

There were two other major challenges for Smith in terms of Regan. The first was the branding that appears on her stomach during the possession; the second was the 360-degree head spin the girl undertakes. For the branding, during which the words 'help me' appear to rise on Regan's torso (a similar instance had appeared in the 1949 Maryland case where the words 'Hell', 'spite' and the numbers '4,8,10' and '16' are all said to have appeared in the form of raised welts on the young boy's skin), Smith "struggled with all kinds of ideas of what to do there – a mechanical device underneath, a false stomach, those sort of things."

The clue to solving this challenge lay in the munchkins of Oz. "The *Wizard of Oz* was virtually one of the first films to use latex. And usually you use new appliances every day, but the munchkins and so forth, they had rather crude appliances, and they would use them for about a week at a time. They would clean them every day and that chore was given to an apprentice, someone's relative I think, who wasn't liked much. So the make-up guys decided to play a joke on him. He would normally collect all the munchkin pieces every day and he would pour out a pail of acetone to clean them. They switched the label on the solvent can and they put the acetone label on a cane of carbon tet, which is petroleum distillate, and any petroleum distillate will attack rubber. And foam latex will virtually explode – it'll suddenly be twice its size if you put it in petroleum distillate. So here's this innocent young lad who takes his box full of appliances and dumps them into this pail of carbon tet, and they practically exploded, to his great amazement and terror.

"As soon as I heard that story I ran and got a piece of foam latex, and tried it out. This was years before *The Exorcist*. But I remembered this and I thought if I can only use that, I could take foam latex and I would paint on it with some cleaning fluid, and it would make a wonderful ridge. The script called for it to be a red welt and I said 'I can't do the colour thing, but maybe I can make it swell up three dimensionally.'" Smith experimented with various solvents on latex before settling on a basic cleaning fluid that left no trace when it dried. "This finally gave me the idea – what happened if we did the welts first, let them dry out with fans, and then reverse the film? The words would appear to be rising up, rather than going away. So that's what we did." Smith used a flameless heatgun, with Blair's pyjamas starched and pinned to her side to avoid the wind from the gun showing.

The head-turning moment required Smith, in collaboration with special effects man Marcel Vercoutere, to build a full-size dummy of Blair. "Dick took a full body cast of Linda," says Vercoutere. "And then after the body cast turned out really well, then we sat down together and Dick says 'If you do everything on the inside, I'll do everything on the outside.'"

Smith built the dummy out of latex-filled polyurethane foam. "No make-up artist at that time had had any experience at doing any mechanical devices," remembers Smith. "I could build the whole dummy – that was fine – but I didn't know how to activate eyeballs. Now this was a very primitive set-up compared to what we have today. All they had to do was go back and forth and side to side. So Marcel provided a servo mechanism that's used in model aeroplane flying – very basic. So I created the dummy and the eyeballs and put in a rig, and then he put in this little servo motor that's radio controlled and that lets you move the eyeballs from side to side. The other thing was the head, which had to turn around backwards. He proposed to do it in a very simple way, which was to put in a long flexible shaft, and he ran this up through the dummy's rear end, through the torso and up to the neck area. Then it connected with the head which I made with a smooth cut across the neck, so when it rotated there would be a crack, but it would all fit neatly together and the edges would be hardly noticeable. So he had a big crank on the end of this shaft and he ran this thing under the bed to where he could lie there and crank the thing. So it was very simple."

"It was frightening; it was so alive," Vercoutere revealed to Mark Kermode. "In fact, I didn't want to call it a dummy. I quit calling it a dummy because it was embarrassing. I said 'I don't want to call you a dummy.' I just called it 'Linda'.

"The one other thing he added for the second appearance of the dummy in the middle of the exorcism," adds Smith, "was it needed to appear to be breathing. So Marcel ran a tube up through the body of the thing to the mouth and we cut small spaces below the teeth, and he could run smoke through this thing and make it look like this thing was breathing and the smoke was condensing."

To test the effectiveness of their creation Vercoutere took 'Linda' for a ride in a New York city taxi cab. 'She' sat on the front seat. When the cab pulled up to another car, people would look over at the dummy. Vercoutere would spin the head round and then quickly drive off.

During the lengthy months of production, Smith, who realised it wasn't safe to leave the dummy at the studio overnight, would take it home with him, again placing it on the front seat of his car, raising more than a few eyebrows from other drivers. "This was a small studio in New York and they're notorious for not being very secure. And I'd left it there one night in the storage room, supposedly locked up, and I came back to find somebody had put some graffiti on the body. It was a warning that it could be tampered with, so from then on I took it home every night in the front seat of my car, driving up the west side highway which is dense with rush hour traffic. And I had a few rather amusing episodes of people driving alongside me and suddenly seeing this strange thing in the car, and the head would sometimes swing around because it moved freely. And I could see in my mirror the frantic efforts of people trying to catch up to get another look. And then when I parked it in my living room, for a while my wife and I would startle ourselves in the morning when we came down half asleep."

While Regan's make-up was by far the most noticeable in the movie, the work required to age forty-three-year-old Max von Sydow into the elderly Father Merrin was by far the most complex. The process took three hours to achieve, with foam latex pieces applied to the actor's face, covering virtually the whole sides of his face, his upper lip, his chin and Adam's apple; this in turn being covered with a heavy, rubber-based greasepaint make-up over the top. In working on the actor's eyes, neck and hands, Smith built on the techniques he had used the year before in ageing Marlon Brando for *The Godfather*, covering these areas with a liquid latex formula applied with a sponge.

"Part of Max's age was what we call old-age stipple or stretch latex. And it's a old-age latex formula that you pat or stipple onto the skin while it's wet. You then stretch the skin contrary to its normal movement, and you dry it with a hairdryer, and when you dry it, it's made the skin less flexible so it wrinkles. I had that all on Max's neck, under his eyes and so forth." Von Sydow's make-up was particularly problematic for Smith when the crew relocated to Iraq to shoot the prologue. With the temperature at 115 degrees in the shade, Smith developed some new latex formulas that were virtually waterproof and therefore able to stand up to the intense heat and perspiration.

"The funny thing is that when *The Exorcist* was released," von Sydow recalled "The critics wrote all about Linda Blair's make-up, but nobody, as far as I know, mentioned my make-up at all, which is a wonderful way of telling it was realistic. They probably thought I was that old."

PROJECTILE VOMITING PEA SOUP –
A DICK SMITH HOW-TO GUIDE

One of the most memorable and notorious images of *The
Exorcist* was the moment where projectile vomiting made
screen history. Regan's repulsive expulsion made audiences recoil,
even though that same audience was quick to cotton on to the fact
that the bile-like substance was, in fact, pea soup. Dick Smith recalls
everything you wanted to know about projectile expunging canned
goods, but were afraid to ask: "I thought it would be simple. What
you do is you run a tube in on the corner of the left side of her mouth
and you shoot it three-quarters from her right side, and you cover the
tube up with an appliance so it's not really noticeable. But was that
good enough for Billy? Oh, no. He said 'The audience will know it's a
cheat. It's got to be full face, right on.' I said 'Billy, how can I get a
tube in her mouth if it's full face.' 'Well, you gotta do it.' I have great
admiration for what he did on that film. Although he was tough and
perfectionist, he got it, he made us do it, and that was right. He had
no diplomacy in his body or soul; he would criticise things brutally,
but as Ellen Burstyn said, if Billy said he liked a performance, you
knew he liked a performance because he never kidded around, he
never flattered, he never tried to make you feel good. So, in a way, it
was a positive thing. But we did have fights. When he came to the
film he wanted, he was immovable, and it could be painful.

Linda Blair and performing tongue

"So here I was faced with what I thought was an impossible problem and I realised I had no experience with doing any mechanical things, so it was a baptism into this entirely new world. I knew something about plastics and I had some thin sheets of a thermo-plastic, which means that it softens in heat. And I remember seeing something about vacu-forming and so forth, so I took these thin sheets and quickly pressed them and pulled them over the side of a life mask of Eileen Dietz, not Linda. And what I had done also in making this particular life mask, I had made these rounded broad hooks that would fit into the corners of the mouth. And before taking the life mask, I had put a hook in each side of her mouth and had her keep her mouth slightly open. And with adhesive tape I had pulled these hooks, and therefore the corners of her mouth, a fair amount. And I taped it back near the ear. Then I'd made the life mask.

"So I have this mask with the face somewhat distorted and the mouth corners open half a inch, so I run this plastic over the sides of the mouth. It's like a sixteenth of an inch thick and I heat-form it so it goes to the corner of the mouth, and I bend it in slightly to duplicate that soft, rounded hook that went into the corner of the mouth originally to hold it. So I make one, and then I build up a strip about three-quarters of an inch wide, out of clay that is going to form a hollow space, again about a sixteenth of an inch thick. Then I vacu-form another piece of plastic on the same path exactly but on top of this rise. So now I have two pieces of vacu-formed plastic that are virtually sandwiched together, but the top one is lifted away from the underneath one so there's this narrow empty space between the two of them. So I do both sides, then I take dental acrylic, which is a wonderful fast-curing plastic that you can mould in almost any shape you want. So I fit a short, round plastic tube between these two side sheets and I tie it in with this dental acrylic. At the other end, back by the ear, I add in another plastic tube to which a rubber tube can be squeezed on. So now I have an apparatus that will fit in the mouth. It doesn't bulge out on the cheeks more than a quarter of an inch or so. The tube that crosses inside the mouth is like a horse's bit and that is detachable. It's a device I've created that can spray pea soup.

"Bill said 'I don't want just a stream of water, I want it more like a garden hose.' And it's hard to make a thing spray in a broad flow in a small place. But it all works fine. Then I have to make a mask to fit over the lower portion of the face to fit it all. That's not hard to do. I duplicate the monster make-up and the rest of the make-up is done. But poor Eileen Dietz has to have this thing in her mouth for hours while this is all glued on. This is why we spared Linda Blair this torture. I rigged up a saliva extraction machine so we could keep her from choking on her own saliva, and to keep her as comfortable as possible, and she was a good sport.

"The irony of all this was it was considered a great success. It was used for the spray that was supposed to hit Karras, and also later on when she lies semi-dormant when Max von Sydow's there, a slow stream of this thick pea soup came out of her mouth on to the pillow. It wasn't until years later that I found out in the editing, Billy had cut out the garden hose spray of vomit because he changed his mind. I think what happened was he got such a great reaction shot on Karras, which was unintentional [Vercoutere's aim was, in fact, off causing him to hit Jason Miller in the face as opposed to on his sweater] and they matted in the vomit as an optical. I thought, 'Gee that looks really great' and we were very pleased with my invention. But the only time it's actually used in the film is the slow flow on the pillow."

With the pea soup on the boil, Friedkin was ready to begin filming *The Exorcist*.

FILMING THE EXORCIST

"**I**t was a realistic film about inexplicable things," says Billy Friedkin, explaining the philosophy behind his approach to *The Exorcist*. "Now those are two almost diametrically opposed notions, but I felt that this story could contain them together – that I could make a film that was realistic, that was not hokey, that didn't look like a Hammer horror film or an Edgar Allen Poe adaptation, with all of its distance from contemporary life. I felt if I could ground this film in contemporary life, yet at the same time, realising that what I'm dealing with in terms of the mysterious illness of the child and medical science's inability to cope with it, as an inexplicable event, then that would be a wonderful combination that I hadn't really seen too much before.

"*2001* was one example of that. There are not many others – realistic films about inexplicable things. It was not unlike what certain of the magic realists were doing in Latin American literature – *One Hundred Years Of Solitude* by Marquez, which I'd been reading – I'd sort of fallen under the spell of the magic realists, so there was that element as well. If you read *One Hundred Years Of Solitude* it is a completely realistic chronicle of this family, during which inexplicable things occur, that we understand given the advance of civilisation and science but which the people who experienced some of those events, had no way of understanding. Like the appearance

Friedkin directing Blair

of ice for the first time in a little town. It would seem like a miracle in the same way that the appearance of a television set in my little apartment where I lived with my mother and father in Chicago was nothing more or less than a miracle. This image coming into our home from where? How? We'd look behind the set – how did it get there? In a way we live with magic all the time, although the magic has some explanation to someone. So I was thinking back then perhaps this is a good way to view *The Exorcist* – as a realistic film about inexplicable events that cannot be interpreted even by the people involved."

Interiors for *The Exorcist* were being constructed at the Ceco Studios in New York. John Robert Lloyd, who had previously worked with Friedkin on *The Night They Raided Minsky's* and *The Boys In The Band*, built the interiors of the MacNeil house, only to find them deemed unsuitable by his director and producer. Friedkin was unsure of certain colour schemes. He wanted the wallpaper in Regan's room to be changed and he wanted all the door frames to be widened to allow for more camera accessibility. Friedkin had originally approved Lloyd's designs, but what he was seeing on early camera tests was not to his satisfaction so Lloyd was promptly fired and Bill Malley was brought in as production designer.

Filming on these interiors, which comprised the action of the majority of the movie, was scheduled for the very beginning of the shoot on 14 August. Bringing Malley in and literally redesigning and rebuilding everything from scratch pushed this start date back to 5 September, then to 18 September and then finally to 25 September.

Warners had budgeted the film at $5 million, allowing eighty-five days for principal photography, divided as eight weeks of mostly interiors in New York, three weeks (largely exteriors) in Georgetown and one week in Iraq. Friedkin didn't consider this unreasonable; he just didn't consider it at all. "I had no idea what the budget was," he says today. "To my memory there was no stated budget to me. I imagine the studio had its own idea of what the budget should be. I've heard figures like $4 1/2 million, anywhere from that to $6 million. But I had no idea what the budget was and I told them: 'I have no idea how much this is gonna cost or how long it's gonna take me to do it. I can tell you how long it will take me to do all the scenes that don't have effects. But the rest of it is, frankly, trial and error.' And they knew that. It wasn't a secret. People are a lot more concerned about those things today where you have these extravagant costs today, where the average film can cost $50 million. But back then we just went out there to make the movie. I had no idea how long it was going to take and I was very upfront about it. I'm certain that the studio had some idea of what they wanted to make it for, and that they became very nervous, edgy, disturbed, frustrated and then angry when it wasn't conforming to their preconceptions."

Despite the problems with its principal sets, *The Exorcist* did in fact begin principal photography in New York on 14 August 1972. There were many reasons for filming in New York as opposed to on the Warner lot in LA, one of which was Friedkin's desire to keep as far away from the studio chiefs as possible. To that extent Blatty was there to act as his buffer. More important, however, were the New York child labour laws which allowed Blair to be on set, with appropriate tutoring, for up to ten or twelve hours a day, as opposed to the mandatory four hours on the West Coast. Given that her make-up took two hours to apply and one to remove, this would leave the young actress available to shoot for only one hour a day, had the film been located in Hollywood.

As the cameras prepared to roll, Friedkin explained his working methods to journalist Peter Travers: "In the process of making a film, I work out a shot-for-shot sequence of how I envision the picture, scene-for-scene. It's all written in a notebook. The script doesn't describe any of the shots. Before each scene I give my notebook to my assistant director, who discusses it with the rest of the crew. When I get to the set they all know what I'm looking for in each scene. For example, scenes forty-one and forty-two in the kitchen have thirteen set-ups. There is a written description of what each set-up should look like and achieve. Some directors diagram it but I find that too cumbersome. It really takes too long to draw so I write it out. In this case, one sentence is worth 500 pictures. You can't show movement in a frame so writing describes it better. I do that for each scene and that way I can see how they all connect."

The first scenes to be shot involved Father Karras visiting his mother in the hospital. They were filmed at the Goldwater Memorial Hospital on Welfare Island, with Vasiliki Maliaros now cast as the mother, after Friedkin had discovered the non-actress in a Greek restaurant in New York. These scenes, and indeed the subplot of Karras and his feelings of inadequacy towards his mother, were crucial to both director and writer/producer. Both men had been deeply devoted to their own mothers. Friedkin had flown his out from Chicago to live with him in Hollywood. As filming began, both men had also recently lost their mothers, something that Blatty was concurrently writing about in his book *I'll Tell Them I Remember You*.

"We have a common background in that we are deeply connected to a mother," Blatty explained to Nat Segaloff. "He is the only child and I, effectively, am the only child because I was the youngest. I would say in my case my grief could be described by an outside observer as neurotic, overdrawn, and one might describe Billy's reaction as the same as mine. And who knows what deep psychic effect it had on both of us." Indeed, when Blatty visited the apartment set of Karras' mother, he remarked that the room should be a lot messier, much like his mother's would have been. Friedkin insisted he was wrong, that it should be extremely neat and ordered. "What he was really saying was '*My* mother would be neat.'"

Before the first shot turned over, it was decided that, having so many priests around and given the film's subject matter, a blessing of the set would not be a bad idea. Father Bill O'Malley, cast as Father Dyer in the film, performed the honours at Goldwater Memorial with a copy of the Roman Ritual in his hand. Subsequent sets and locations would be blessed in a similar way, generally by technical adviser, Father John Nicola.

"He was the man that the Catholic church put forward," explains Friedkin "having published on the subject, as their foremost expert in America on exorcism. I met with him and he sort of indicated to me how this would proceed, how it would be done. And I don't know if he ever suggested to me that we let him bless the set, or if it was my idea, but clearly it became my idea. Why not? If nothing else it was very much in keeping with what we were doing to have those vibrations be present on the set. We weren't doing it because it was chic or anything like that. We were working with all these priests and it seemed like a very good idea to have them perform priestly functions around us. There was no romantic notion to any of that. I have not done it on any of my sets since, but it seemed like a good idea at the time."

With filming now underway, Blatty found his role somewhat sidelined. Consequently, he spent less and less time on set, occupying himself with scouting locations in Georgetown, negotiating the film's way into Iraq and keeping the studio at bay.

"He was totally supportive," Friedkin insists. "I don't think it was ever difficult for him. We had a couple of procedural arguments before we started shooting. They were all petty things, like should Ellen Burstyn have a limousine meet her at the airport in New York when she arrived from California. I said 'yes'; he said 'no.' I said 'You've got to be kidding. She's your star. You're not gonna give her a limousine?' He said 'Well, she can take a cab.' I said 'You're a fucking asshole.' And he said 'Well, that's the way I'm gonna run this picture.' So I said 'You might as well fire me because I'm not gonna treat people that way and I have to deal with them every day.' And he said 'OK, you're fired' and I was fired for about twenty-four hours. And then sanity prevailed and we went onto it. Both Blatty and I were given over to a lot of pettiness in those days. We were completely full of ourselves."

Sanity prevailed apparently only after Friedkin appeared on set with a coterie of legal aid plus agent, all of whom were there to explain to Blatty exactly why he was in no position to fire Friedkin. "I'm the producer of record on the film," Blatty says. "I just wanted to be around watching what they were doing. I asked Warner Brothers to revise my contract to accommodate for that. In other words, they rewrote a clause in the contract that more or less said that I would not be responsible for any overruns at this point. And they made an adjustment in their method of computing my profits. I knew we were going over, but the studio was comfortable. They were well aware of it."

Following the first day's shoot at Goldwater Memorial, Friedkin and crew shot a pivotal scene on the New York subway, where Father Karras is asked for money by a local indigent, uttering the line "Father, could you help an old altar boy? I'm a Catholic", later uttered by the possessed Regan. Although unbilled in the movie, the bum was in fact played by a bum.

"Friedkin and I were coming from a play one night on 57th," Jason Miller recalled to Mark Kermode. "I'll never forget it, 57th and 8th. And this guy Vinnie was bumming money on the corner. And I said 'Bill, that's the guy that should be on the subway.' Bill went over to him and said 'You wanna be in a movie?' 'Yeah, I'll be in a movie. What do you want me to do?' So the next day we sent six cases of beer, got a limo and he had all his buddies there and they all piled into the limo and they all came up to the suburb where we were filming. Well, by the time we got to filming he was shit-faced, loaded, out of his mind. We were pouring coffee down him. I said 'Let him do it like that.' And he was pretty good on it. A lot of spontaneous things happened on the making of this film."

A hospital in Queens doubled for the venue of one of Regan's examinations and offered Linda Blair's mother – Elinore – a two-line cameo as a nurse who advises the doctor that Chris MacNeil is on the phone. And just off 11th Avenue a run-down tenement block served as the location, both exterior and interior, of Mrs. Karras' apartment.

Interiors for the Jesuit quarters, where Karras shares a drink or two with Father Dyer after the death of his mother, were filmed at Fordham University, home at that time to Father Thomas Bermingham, whose presence greatly aided the production's access to the university. After rehearsing this scene for several hours and, feeling that it still wasn't working, Miller suggested that he and the neophyte actor try the drinking for real. Friedkin's secretary, Diane Repetto came through with a bottle of Jack Daniels and soon both actor and priest were more than mildly merry and bonding over earnest conversations on the meaning of life. By the time Friedkin found them encamped in his office, the two men had solved any problems they may have had and the scene was shot a few days later.

The delay in set construction did cost the production a key aspect of one scene. Chris MacNeil's party in Georgetown, where Regan tells an astronaut guest "You're going to die up there", before urinating on the carpet, was to have been peopled by a number of real-life celebrities and prominent people. However, due to the constant rescheduling, this idea was abandoned.

Although he was not required in New York for several weeks yet, Max von Sydow flew in from Sweden during the early days of filming to spend forty-eight hours with make-up man Dick Smith, perfecting the difficult make-ups required in ageing the forty-three-year-old. The actor was, at the time, also appearing with the Royal Repertory Theatre in Oslo and planned to commute between this and the set of *The Exorcist*.

During the first few days of filming an accident occurred, the significance of which was to figure prominently in what came to be seen as the "curse" of *The Exorcist*. During an early break from filming, Jason Miller was relaxing at the beach with his three children. The youngest, Jordan, was playing in the sand when a motorcycle appeared from over a sand dune, crashing into the boy. Only by waving down a police helicopter did Miller manage to get an ambulance and young Jordan was rushed to Rockaway Hospital. For the next ten days he lay in critical condition, a matter exacerbated by the fact that the boy had undergone critical neurosurgery the year before. Father Thomas Bermingham maintained a vigil by his side throughout that ten days, but his father was forced to move between the hospital and the set, shooting the pivotal emotional scenes with his screen mother at the same time as his own son lay in the hospital, his future uncertain. After ten days, Jordan made a full recovery, but the accident signalled the beginnings of a mythology that would grow around the movie, forever blurring the lines between the real and the supernatural, the actuality and the hype.

With the majority of the New York exteriors complete, the cast and crew of *The Exorcist* repaired to the story's spiritual home – Georgetown in Washington. Georgetown University was where Blatty had first learned of the 1949 exorcism that eventually inspired his book; it was only fitting that the first Georgetown-set scenes in the film would take place at that very location, with Jack MacGowran's lush-like director Burke Dennings filming Chris MacNeil's latest starring role on campus. (The scenes were shot on the steps of the campus' Healy Hall.) Appropriately, Blatty played the producer of this film within a film, *Crash Course*.

It was whilst on location at the university campus that Blatty finally discovered the name of the boy involved in the 1949 Maryland exorcism. "Father Bowdern – the exorcist – had kept a daily diary during the course of the exorcism which lasted approximately three months," explains Blatty, referring to the same diary no doubt that Jason Miller had earlier viewed. "At the end of the day he would write up his account and he would have every person who had been assisting in the room write their account, verifying that these things had actually happened. I never was allowed to get my hands on the diary. However, while we were filming on the campus of Georgetown university, I went up to the library and got into the stacks and went rummaging around, and what did i find? I found index cards referencing the 1949 case. And I hauled them all out and one of them was a précis of the events – fairly accurate – but I couldn't believe my eyes because there was the name of the boy and there was his address – right there. Well, I crossed them out in heavy marker pen. But I was often tempted to go and find him, but I never did."

Before the rest of the crew arrived, Blatty and associate producer David Salven spent several weeks in Georgetown scouting locations. Key among these was the MacNeil house. For this they chose 3600 Prospect Street, the home of Washington socialite Florence Mahoney. The house bordered on a steep set of steps – soon dubbed by the production (and for all time) the 'Hitchcock Steps' – that, as in Blatty's book, led down to the nearby M Street.

"It's amazing how Blatty set this particular story in a place that does exist," Friedkin said at the time. "He caught the life and feelings of that place which certainly influence all the characters in the story. The places were all there and quite accessible. Georgetown has never appeared in a feature film but it has marvellous qualities for this type of film." Despite the appropriateness of the Mahoney house, the production crew added the façade of a new wing, connecting the property to the steps. This allowed Regan's bedroom window to directly overlook them – a vital aspect for the story given that two characters (Dennings and Karras) are pushed and/or jump from the window to the steps below.

The exterior of the Mahoney house, both real and movie-imagined, provided the locale for what remains the single most memorable image from the movie – Father Merrin's arrival – later used as the poster art and key trailer image for the film. For this deeply chilling image, Friedkin cleverly reversed the standard precepts of characters caught in a battle of good versus evil, in that the 'hero' (for want of a better word) is the mysterious figure in black, while the 'villain' lies within the white light emanating from Regan's bedroom window. It's a challenging image and one for which Friedkin found his inspiration in the works of French surrealist Rene Magritte.

"The inspiration for it was Magritte's *Empire Of Light*," the director explains. "The shot is not a duplicate of *Empire Of Light* but what you have basically in the bottom half of the painting is a night scene, some very ominous trees and a street lamp lit in front of a house, and yet the sky is filled with light. So my equivalent of the sky filled with daylight at the top of the frame and the bottom of the frame being a house and its environs at night, was to have an unearthly light shining out of the girl's window picking up Merrin as he gets out of the taxi cab. It's a surrealistic moment with the emphasis on realistic."

The scene required three city blocks to be isolated and fogged in with fog machines, something that proved problematic as unseasonable winds kept blowing the effect away. Nonetheless, the scene did have an immediate impact. "We had to get permits to fog in three city blocks," special effects man Marcel Vercoutere recalled. "Then with all the arc lights, I remember everyone was alerted on our side, but on the other side of the Markee bridge, which is Virginia, lo and behold they thought Georgetown was on fire. So they came from another state, across the bridge, with their ladders and fire trucks. We were lit up so bright, they could see us for miles."

Knowing that his dailies were being viewed by the Warner Brothers chiefs, this famous scene almost featured another actor in the Merrin role – none other than Groucho Marx. Blatty knew Marx from his appearance on the latter's quiz show *You Take Your Pick*, and his many years as a comedy screenwriter. He recalled the incident for Friedkin biographer Nat Segaloff: "On the Friday before the Monday we were to shoot events at the MacNeil house, beginning with the arrival of Father Merrin. Billy and I were having dinner. Over the wine I said 'Wouldn't it be funny if, instead of Max von Sydow showing up at the door, removing his hat and saying "Mrs MacNeil, I'm Father Merrin," it was Joe Fretwell, the film's costume designer, who speaks with a southern accent?' And Billy said 'What if it were Groucho Marx?' I said 'Groucho's in town and he's a friend of mine. Would you actually do this?' The plan was that not only would he appear at the door – he'd take his hat off and it's Groucho Marx – but that Jason Miller would precede Groucho into the room and we'd have Eileen Dietz as the demon, tied to the bed. And when she screamed a certain ten-letter obscenity, the duck [a regular prop from Groucho's quiz show] would come down."

Groucho, sadly, proved unavailable at the last minute, leaving von Sydow to shoot one of the indelible images of modern cinema as a solo. The actor travelled back from Oslo to film this key sequence in Georgetown and the following day, he received a telegram informing him that his brother had unexpectedly passed away. Again, this incident would later find its way into the enduring myth of the curse of *The Exorcist*. Indeed, this fondness for all things potentially supernatural was something that many of the principals at the time were only too willing to play around with, often to almost ridiculous lengths, witness Ellen Burstyn's contemporary account of filming, chalking up Billy Friedkin's directorial prowess as borderline uncanny.

"We did a scene in Washington where Father Karras and Chris are walking down a path. The cameras were way at the bottom of a hill, a half-block away. As we walked down the hill, extras were positioned all around us. After one take Billy came to give us some direction. He told me what I was thinking on a line of Jason's and why he didn't want me to think that way. Then he told Jason what he was doing wrong on the same line. He also told an extra in the background he was smiling as he was walking and that he shouldn't be. He further instructed an extra – in the foreground – that his colour was too bright and that he would have to be taken out of the scene. I mean, Billy was a half-block away yet he was seeing my thoughts and all of this other stuff. This is not humanly possible! It happened again. This time the scene was the university and there were 500 extras. I walked on the scene and Billy said 'Ellen, I've never seen those black pumps before.' I have twenty-two changes of hats, scarves, gloves and other things yet he noticed a pair of new black shoes. That is so spooky."

In the 1998 BBC documentary on the movie *The Fear Of God*, Burstyn claimed "during the course of filming there were nine deaths, which is an enormous amount of deaths, connected with the film."

One of the deaths that took place on camera was Father Karras's plunge down the Hitchcock steps. Special effects man Marcel Vercoutere lined all ninety-seven steps with rubber for the stuntman to hurl himself down over two takes. (The Georgetown locals were so keen to see the stunts that local and adjacent houses were renting out roof space for $5 a head to get a good view of the action.) The stunt was filmed in its entirety twice. "I asked the stunt man – Charlie Walters – how he did it," Jason Miller recalled for the BBC. "And he said 'Zen . . . complete and total non-resistance. My body becomes totally relaxed.' And he did. He stood there before he did it, like three minutes before he went into a trance. He truly could have broken his neck, that's how dangerous the stunt was."

"Before he took off," explained effects man Marcel Vercoutere of his contribution to the stuntman's fall, "I rolled up his sweater at the back and took a big plastic bag and fixed it on with gaffer tape. I just totally filled it up with blood, right up to the top, and before he went I cut it. So every time he turned over, blood came out the back of his neck. And when he ended up at the bottom, his head was twisted and it just kept filling up this pool down there. And I said 'Wow' and it just kept coming."

The reaction to this, as the crowd gathers round Karras and Dyer fights his way through to administer the last rites to his friend, was filmed well into the early hours of the morning and saw Friedkin employing a 'technique' he hadn't used since *The People Versus Paul Crump*. In front of his crew, Jason Miller and numerous extras, Friedkin slapped Father William O'Malley hard across the face.

"He did it fifteen times before I slapped him," the filmmaker explains, "And I realised that even in the realistic moment of delivering last rites – something that he knew – to his friend, he couldn't act it. I then had to create a moment of chaos for him, which produced the result, which it often and generally does. It's such a shocking thing to do. I think I've done it three times in thirty years and that's one of them. (The other incidents being the aforementioned Paul Crump and a scene, later deleted from *To Live And Die In L.A*, where Friedkin slapped actor John Pankow.) It's not something that you want to do or gloat over or enjoy. But there's often no other way."

Unit Publicist Howard Newman recalled the incident in detail: "After going through the scene about fifteen different times, Billy Friedkin called O'Malley aside and told the priest he wasn't getting the expression of fear in his face he had hoped to capture in the scene. Even priests can lose their patience and the weary O'Malley pleaded with the director: 'Billy, it's two in the morning. When you've seen your best friend die fifteen times in one night, you've really got to pull the emotions out of your guts.' 'Do you trust me?' asked Friedkin. The priest nodded. Friedkin stepped out of hearing range to talk with the soundman and cameraman. He then came back to O'Malley and spoke to him quietly for a few seconds, again asking the priest if he trusted him. The priest assured him again without really understanding what the director was up to. Friedkin then nodded to the soundman, who yelled 'speed', just as the cameraman boomed 'rolling.' With that Friedkin hauled off and belted O'Malley right across the face. Stunned, the priest turned around and went through the scene a final time. With a trembling voice, O'Malley absolved Karras for the last time, his hands shaking and tears welling up in his eyes. As Karras died, O'Malley threw himself down on the bloody corpse sobbing uncontrollably. 'Cut!' yelled the delighted Friedkin, who ran over to the shaken priest, grabbing him up in his arms and planting a big kiss right where he had struck him."

"He belted me right across the chops and backed off," Father O'Malley told the BBC. "And I went into the scene. And if you look at it carefully, my hand is shaking. I wasn't making my hand go like that. That was sheer nerve juice. Then Billy bounded over and he gave me a kiss right on the mush, and a stage hand handed me a glass of scotch and I thought well, I'm home free now. That was a memorable night – a really memorable night." Friedkin adds, "What do you do to get an effect on screen? Whatever it takes."

Additional filming in Georgetown took place in the small Dahlgren Chapel, a university-based site dating back to 1892. Here, Friedkin shot Jason Miller delivering the mass (Father O'Malley acted as technical adviser) and the set-up to the desecration scenes. The actual close-ups of the desecrated statues were filmed back in the New York studios to avoid offending any members of the church.

During the Georgetown shoot, Cliff Chieffo, the university liaison with the production, decided to set up a basketball game between the faculty members and the cast and crew of the movie, the latter known as Exorcists, the former as Demons. (This game later provided the inspiration for the title of Blatty's satirical 1996 novel *Demons Five, Exorcists Nothing*.) Friedkin, an avid basketball watcher, who had harboured dreams of becoming a pro player back in his adolescence, led The Exorcists, alongside Jason Miller and numerous teamsters. They played valiantly, but eventually lost out to The Demons with a score of forty-five to forty-four. *The Washington Star* covered the game on its sports pages.

Before filming concluded in Georgetown, Lee J. Cobb paid a PR visit to the local chief of police – Jerry Wilson – to deliver a $5,000 cheque made payable to the Patrolmen's Benevolent Fund, a customary means of a film production showing its gratitude for the police assistance they received whilst filming on location. Then it was back to New York and time to bring the Devil to life.

Despite the last minute changes in the principal sets and the necessity to juggle the shooting schedule to accommodate that, *The Exorcist* had, up until this point, still been a relatively easy shoot. 'Easy' in that it was more or less on time, more or less on budget, and everyone was more than pleased by what they were seeing in the rushes. On the production's return to Ceco Studios all that was to change. What followed had little or nothing to do with any so-called curse. Billy Friedkin had said right from the start that getting Blatty's novel on screen in an anyway believable form was going to be a process of trial and error. When the movie was still in principal photography six months later and its budget had doubled, everyone believed him.

It was by no means a case of mismanagement or egos running rampant; the shooting schedule for *The Exorcist* had simply left all the potentially difficult work until this time, affording Dick Smith much needed time to work on his make-up and to prepare the numerous appliances that would be required during the shooting, and allowing special effects man Marcel Vercoutere time to work out the logistics of the numerous bed-flying, breath-seeing effects that would appear on screen in the film's final act – the exorcism itself. The production team were back in New York and they would be there for a while.

Away from the technical aspects, now was really the time for Linda Blair to come into her own. Over the coming months she would be tied to her bed, thrown around her bed, levitated above her bed, spew pea soup over her bed, spend hours having an increasingly complex, increasingly grotesque make-up applied to her pretty teenage features, and throughout all this she was expected to deliver a performance that must move from the vile to the vulnerable.

"I treated Linda as I would an adult," says Friedkin, when asked if he ever worried about what he was exposing the young actress to. "I had a great relationship with Linda. I was a surrogate father for her, and a good father in that I treated her like a real person and I think she appreciated that. I mean I was conscious she was a child but she had tremendous mental capacity, an ability to process information and she was totally together. So I didn't need to treat her like a baby. And I made the whole thing a game for her so that all of this outrageous stuff was a game. And at the end of each scene where she was the demon, there are photographs of Linda sitting there in demon make-up with the prop man offering her a milkshake. We all made it a game for her. It was a very good crew; they were very respectful of her. We all liked each other and they all loved Linda. It was a family for her. And interestingly, her mother and father were separated and undergoing problems that Linda was conscious of. And I don't know if she realises this – I'm sure she does – in a way her coming to the set every day was a kind of escape from the pressures of her family life. She came into another family where she had responsibility and where everyone was there to be concerned about her needs and well being."

"I was extremely concerned what effect this would all have on the girl," Blatty concurs. "And I can tell you, however, that whenever we were coming up on the dicey scenes, all the crew would sort of tiptoe around on days when we were doing those scenes. And Linda Blair's reaction after every take was that she would giggle. She was amused by it."

"When we got to the demon stages," Blair explained to Kermode, "Billy would take me up into his office and he'd say 'OK, now here's a piece of paper that has tomorrow's dialogue on. This is the new dialogue.' And I would sit on the couch and I'd read it and I'd go 'I can't say that.' And he'd say 'Yeah, you can.' He has a way of making people do things. Because it was a closed set there was never more than four or five people on the set while filming. The guys just got used to looking at me. I mean, I was just part of the set. So the fact that there were very few people allowed me to say the dialogue that I was being asked to say. No one was allowed to laugh. And they were never allowed to make me feel uncomfortable. I had to do what I had to do."

Dick Smith had already done what he had to do. Or at least he thought he had. Friedkin had agreed his designs for the demon make-up weeks before, allowing the make-up artist plenty of time to make the numerous appliances. This is a laborious process with each foam latex 'mask' taking up to six hours to bake in its mould, thus allowing Smith to generally make only two a day. For each day of filming that required a demon make-up, a new 'mask' was needed.

The first scene to involve this make-up – in its earliest manifestation – was when Regan is hypnotised in her bedroom by a psychiatrist. "In the course of the action Regan grabs him by the balls," recalls Smith "And causes great consternation amongst all attending. That was supposed to be a subtle version of that make-up. And we shot the scene and we screened it and Billy said 'This is not going to work.' I, at first, was rather disappointed and argued with him because I thought it was a good make-up, and it *was* a good make-up. But Billy was right and I came to see that because the dialogue became impossible with her appearing so changed. She wasn't a little girl anymore; she was some slightly, but definitely changed, more adult-looking creature. So then I had to start another series of tests, and by this time the reference material I was using was getting pretty thin, and I was desperate, trying to think of other possible concepts. Billy kept harking on the original exorcism in which it was said that the little boy had gashes and cuts and scratches on his face and body, which supposedly could not have been self inflicted. I was opposed to that because I think blood and gore is a cheap way to do horror, so on principle I didn't want to get into that."

Smith showed Friedkin a still of Claude Rains as the Phantom of the Opera, the asymmetricality of the face appealing to the director. "Billy wanted to keep everyone guessing as to whether she was truly possessed or whether it was just an aberration of some sort. With my original make-up, there would have been no question.

"Nevertheless, during this next series of tests I did a few other versions," Smith continues. "One of them, which I rather liked, I later used in *The Heretic [Exorcist II]* on the little black boy. I did a couple with cuts and bleeding and things like that, and out of that there were another five or six that we tested. Out of that Billy thought that the scratches and the blood were the best way to go. What I then did was to take bits and pieces that I thought were successful from all the tests and combine them."

Regan's face now featured a number of cuts and gashes, Friedkin's idea being that these could easily be seen as self-inflicted wounds thus adding to the debate over the validity of Regan's possession. Smith added appliances to lose the cupid's bow look of Blair's mouth. (False teeth were to be used, but were quickly abandoned as they affected her delivery.) Blair's own teeth were instead painted with tooth enamel to make them look rotten and decayed.

"As she progressed, I used a lot of black and blue coloration," Smith continues "To make her look sick and gaunt. Her skin was made pale and jaundiced. And lastly, we used contact lenses – not at the beginning, but as she progressed. I had three sets of contact lenses made as a progression, starting with a rather mild change with yellow green irises with slightly smaller pupils, and we found unless you shot really tight close-ups with really strong lighting, only the last pair really showed a difference. It was my first experience with this kind of situation as far as eyes are concerned and I learned that only really strong changes in the coloration of the eyes will really read on screen. So we only used the final and more extreme set, which had small pupils which made the iris more prominent, and it also looked a little weird. You either go for dilated pupils or you go for the little pinpoint kind of pupils, and that gives a weird, unusual look. They were the old fashioned hard lenses. Now it's soft lenses for everything. Linda couldn't get used to them so I had to use anaesthetising drops in her eyes before putting them in. And they would only last so long. The important point is that we got closer and closer to Linda herself," recalled Smith. "And therefore it became more believable. She was really almost recognisable. At least it was the most moderate kind of transformation we could do."

Friedkin's desire to redesign the previously approved look of Regan led to Dick Smith scrapping the vast majority of the prosthetics he had been making for several months before production began. "All that work went down the drain," he says. "Billy had to change his shooting schedule since we couldn't go on with these until I made the changes. It was several weeks before we were able to go further with it. I hired a very talented young man who had written to me when he was a teenager. I had so much work to do I brought him in from Hollywood. His name was Rick Baker. Rick now has five Academy Awards and a huge, huge make-up studio with nearly a hundred people employed there. That's what can happen in twenty-five years in this crazy business."

Smith's work was not only immensely time-consuming, but largely directed at a teenage girl, and they are not always the most patient of creatures. "She was remarkable throughout the whole thing," he recalls. "Linda was quite an adult young lady. Her mother came most of the time and she was very good. She wasn't a stage mother; she kept in the background and didn't interfere with anything – didn't hover. Linda was pretty much on her own. She was really very, very patient. Of course it was boring for her to sit for two hours in the morning while this stuff was put on. So she asked if she could have a television set. So what we did was put a small set on a shelf on the wall behind her, so she could look in the make-up mirror and see the set."

Blair's choice of programming at the time was Sally Field's sixties sitcom *The Flying Nun*. "The only problem was I stand on the person's right side when I'm making them up, which is fine when I'm making up their right side. But when I have to make up their left side, I lean in front of them and it would block her view of *The Flying Nun*.

So she would then move her head further to her left and I would have to lean further, and we'd end up playing games dodging each other to try and finish the make-up."

"God bless Dick Smith," continued Linda Blair. "Nothing could've prepared anybody for what that experience was going to be. Maybe an adult might have taken better to it. I was always very good about it. Billy's decision was he didn't want it to look like I was wearing a mask so Dick Smith would continue to chip away at the pieces and there were several different (prosthetic) pieces on my face. Then there was the numbing drops. How good can that be for the eyes? I went through probably three months of having numbing drops put in my eyes. To this day I still can't wear contacts. It was a very painful process."

Alongside the physical discomfort of her new demonic look, and occasional interruptions to Sally Field's early morning aeronautics, Blair faced another on-set indignity – she hated pea soup. "She was at that stage where even the word 'vomit' was distasteful to her," recalls Dick Smith. "She would say 'upchuck' or something like that. Myself and the special effects guy Marcel Vercoutere had decided that plain pea soup would be the best substitute for the colour and texture required. And this he would pump through his apparatus and my mouth apparatus. Linda hated pea soup and the smell of it, so I went to great pains to try to make it easier for her, and I concocted a harmless substitute for pea soup that had no odour and tried that out. It was all in vain because it had to be on her costume. She just didn't like the sight of it. So, as it didn't make any difference, we went back to pea soup."

Among the more unusual jobs Smith found himself doing on *The Exorcist* was teaching its teenage star to spit. "She was supposed to spit a big gob of phlegm. And of course it doesn't come naturally for people to spit like they'd been chewing tobacco all day. And so one day I spent around two hours in the make-up room, which had a sink at one end of the room. Backing off six paces or so, I would try and teach her how to spit. I prepared some gloppy stuff that was harmless and I would demonstrate. I'm no tobacco chewer, but I would manage. But she never could learn it, so we gave up on that. But I thought it was kind of hilarious that this was part of my task as a make-up artist to try and teach a young lady to spit."

Like many others on the production, Smith's initial concerns over certain scenes and events that Blair would have to go through were quickly allayed by the young actress's winning personality and level headedness. "The thing I think concerned a lot of people, including myself, were the scenes where she had to say really obscene language. And in fact even the stage hands, when she would say these things, were kind of shocked – it coming out of the mouth of this little girl, even if she was in make-up. I think I had a very good relationship with Linda; we talked a lot – she loved horses and I had worked in a stable once, and so forth. So I asked her one day 'Linda, how do you feel when you say these awful things?' And she said 'Oh, it's not me, it's Regan.' And that divorcing herself from the character she was playing, I thought, was a very good way to deal with it. I assumed that was her idea at the time but it may have been Ellen Burstyn's. Ellen was like a mother to her on the set. She was really good with her and they developed a really close relationship that was very supportive for Linda. And that was very important because she wasn't very experienced with acting and Ellen gave her a lot of help with that, but it also gave her a great moral support. I was very concerned of course, because I'd worked with a lot of child actors and I had seen little monsters. Like a little guy around twelve or younger boss the parents around in a horrible way and the parents just kind of grovelling for their breadwinner. And I'd also worked with Patty Duke who'd had a terrible childhood, which she told me all about. But I really think that when Linda left the film she hadn't been damaged psychologically in any way. All she wanted to do was get back to her horses and her family and her school, and that sort of thing.

"I do think that afterwards – this is only my own guess – but she had problems. And I think it was the agents, whoever they were. I don't mean to imply any evil or any bad motives on behalf of the agents but agents are, after all, trying to get jobs for their clients and to get their percentage. I feel they are like modern Fagins when it comes to children. I feel they are exploitative; I feel that they kept tempting and pushing Linda into things that took her away from her home life and put her into the Hollywood world at a very young age. And to live that life, not just for one year, but for the rest of her teenage, formative years, is very destructive and inevitably causes harm, and I think it did. But fortunately, she's a strong young lady and has recovered. And I'm very happy for that."

Before beginning production, Friedkin needed to know that the elaborate effects required for the final exorcism could actually be achieved in the controlled environs of a studio set. He recruited special effects man Marcel Vercoutere and initially sent him to New York to meet with a magician who specialised in levitation. "All the things that he showed me could not possibly be shot on a set," Vercoutere explained to journalist Kermode "because you had to hide it with this and hide it with that. So I turned round and came back to California. Then I sat there with Billy and he said 'They don't want to do the film because they think it can't be done. So I'm gonna send you to New York again and meet with his make-up man, Dick Smith, and I want you to get together with him and set up this bedroom scene of the exorcism and we're gonna shoot it with extras, and if it looks like we might be able to get away with it, we're going with it.' "

Vercoutere and Smith shot a test of the final scene over a period of three days. Friedkin was suitably impressed. Vercoutere's contribution to *The Exorcist* was to prove immeasurable, involving everything from levitating beds to throwing Linda Blair around, from reducing her bedroom to a sub-zero chamber to keeping the pea soup warm.

Vercoutere began by building three identical beds for Regan, each rigged for a specific effect. "All the beds were made out of steel tubing. The floating bed was done by weights and a beam that went from the back of the headboard through the wall. It had counter weights on the other side. I had as much weight behind the wall as I did with the bed weight. Then all I had to do was take that up in the centre, up and down – I could do whatever I wanted with the bed levitating. I had two cables coming down the legs. Then I pulled it back down from underneath. So instead of going up, we were actually pulling it down. The bed was trying to fly but it couldn't because I was pulling it back." Vercoutere positioned a roller with wallpaper on it behind the headboard which wound up and down with the bed, effectively covering the hole his equipment protruded through.

Another of his beds was designed to throw Regan about. Vercoutere began by taking a mould of Blair's back and making a brace out of thin metal. Blair would then be laced into this device that was rigged to the bed, and controlled and manipulated by Vercoutere from the other side of the back wall. "I said to Billy 'I would like to get personal. I'd like to get hold of her. If I was the Devil I'd get up and grab her and thrash her. I would let her know.' He said go ahead and do it. So I built a rig in another bed and I had her completely strapped in. I had her. I could throw her up and back and I had her. And I said 'Linda, I gotcha.' "

"The lacing came loose when I was being thrown," recalled the actress to the BBC. "It was manually pumped by some big man on the other side of the wall and the lacing came loose while we were filming and so as I went forward, the piece was coming back. So the dialogue was 'Please make it stop, make it stop, it hurts, it burns' whatever, and I'm having my back pounded and I'm screaming 'it hurts, make it stop' and I didn't know what to do. And somebody thought I yelled 'Billy' but I actually never broke character. And the footage they used in the movie was where I'm crying my eyes out because they're brutally damaging my back, which would not show up for many years later. I've had a horrible time with my back because of that. And I've never gone back to Warner Brothers, never said anything."

"Even though Billy was shooting," Vercoutere adds, "He didn't start printing until she said 'I've had enough.' When she started screaming 'Let me out,' Billy said 'Go.' And that's what worked. She was saying 'let me out' – she really wanted out. She was getting

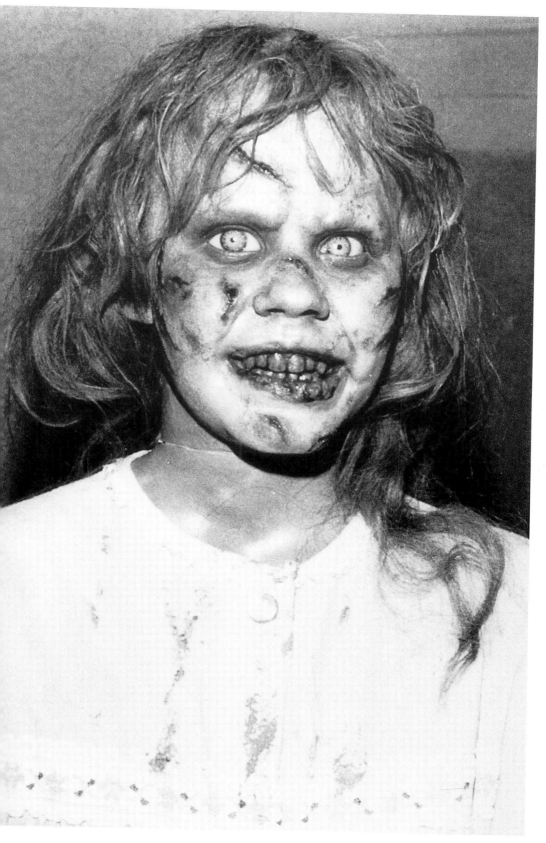

Bill & Billy:
(Above) William Peter Blatty
(Left) William Friedkin

(Above) Ellen Burstyn and Linda Blair before possession
(Below) Jason Miller disproving heat theories about Hell

Projectile vomiting pea soup: state of the art special effects, 1974 style.

(Above) An un-possessed young Linda Blair (Left) A slightly older, un-possessed Linda

(Above) Max von Sydow and Linda Blair in a German publicity still for the original film

(Below) A rare double-showing poster for Exorcist and Exorcist II The Heretic

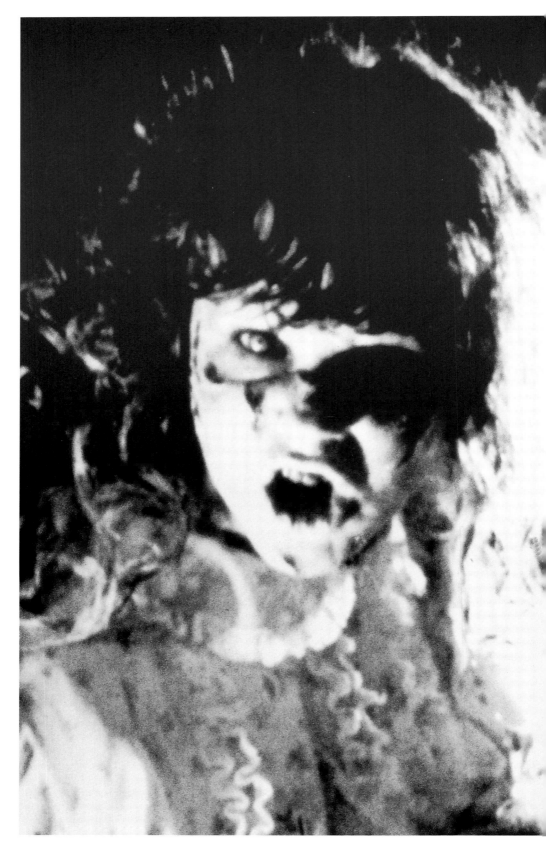

thrashed, you know. But that's what looks good on film. It worked for that."

For several years after the release of *The Exorcist*, Friedkin claimed that the levitation of Blair was achieved using magnetic fields in a manner that he never elaborated on. This was of course Friedkin as consummate showman, determined to maintain the myth of his movie. The effect was in fact a good deal simpler than this – thin piano wire. "I think it was number 8 piano wire. Three threads," Vercoutere says. "Then I rigged the bed so that when she came down into it, the bed recessed, so it looked like all of her weight was coming down into it. I could take her up and pull her around. It was done with counter weights; I had her same weight off-stage so I could work it with one hand. The object was to do it as smoothly as possible."

"Again, it was the mould of my back," Blair continues "which I laid in and from my memory there were three wires to this nice big crucifix above my head. I was always safe. And this was where Owen [Roizman], our director of photography, would spray paint the wires. I was in that rigging for hours because in order to do the levitation scene they had to make sure where the camera was, where the lights were etc., so they could never see a wire. And you cannot see a wire."

Having thrown Blair around with full abandon, Vercoutere was also the man charged with making the actress pee on demand. "I did that using an airplane remote control system," he explains. "I used a thin tank that went on her back, since all the shots were straight on. She had to come straight down the stairs, then through a little alcove and then straight into the living room, where they were playing the piano and singing. So all she had to do was do her number. And then I just kicked on the switch and started it."

The effects expert used warm beer as a urine substitute. "Beer has a nice brownish colour and it foams when it hits," he explained.

Regan's bedroom, however, provided Vercoutere with his greatest challenge. It was constructed on eight pneumatic wheels to create the earthquake-like effect needed during the final exorcism. The cracking ceiling effect was created by moulding plaster cast round mesh wire, which Vercoutere would press down on and stretch, cracking the surface. A similar effect with a cracking door was achieved in the same way, this time using a balsa wood door.

More importantly, Friedkin wanted to see the breath of the actors in the room which, due to the presence of the demon, is now freezing. For this Vercoutere cocooned the set off, using eight inches of fibreglass insulation, effectively isolating a space that was forty feet square by twenty feet high. Above the room he positioned four vast freezing units and refrigerated the set: "They were these huge meat packing plant cooling fans," Blair told Kermode. "And they kept them on all night long and so in the morning it'd be below zero, then they would light the set and it would come up to zero, and then when it would reach something like seventeen degrees above, they'd have to turn the fans back on. We had a sauna outside. I really never, never used the sauna. It was made for all of us. Everyone else got to wear snow suits; I had a night-gown on. There were times I could wear long underwear, there were times I could not. There were times the blankets were on me, many times they were not. Was it cold? Yes. Did I like it? Not much. That's probably why I hate cold so much nowadays." Von Sydow concurs, "It was difficult to act and express emotions when your face was frozen – literally."

"Billy would get the damn thing down to zero fahrenheit," Dick Smith recollects. "It was so cold that one morning we came in and there must have been excess humidity in the air because there was a layer of snow over the whole set. Max and Jason had the worst of it because they just had a suit of thermal underwear under their clerical garbs. Their hands were bare and their heads and everything, so they were really freezing. Linda was sleeping on top of a heated blanket so that helped her a bit. I invented a waterproof paint for her legs so I wouldn't have to retouch them with ordinary wet pancake make-up on the set because it would've been too uncomfortable."

The contact lenses Blair was required to wear also caused problems under these arctic conditions. "I would normally put the lenses in on the outside of this cocoon," says Smith. "I forgot one day and we're just about ready to shoot and someone says 'Are her contacts in?' and I said 'Sorry, I goofed.' And Billy said 'Can you do them here?' because she was in bed and strapped down and ready to go. Now before you put contact lenses in you have to clean them with a cleaning agent. So I'm doing this between my fingers and I think something's broken because I feel this sharp, loose piece. And I look down at it and it's not the lens; it's a little thin piece of ice that's formed from the cleaning solution. So I had to tell them I can't do it and had to take her out. That's how cold it was."

On 31 January 1973, with the production already over schedule, news reached the Ceco Studios that Jack MacGowran had died. The actor had completed his shooting weeks before and had subsequently turned up for a dubbing session with Friedkin, during the time he was performing in Sean O'Casey's *The Plough And The Stars* at the nearby Lincoln Centre. Shortly after this, early one Sunday morning at around 3 a.m., the Ceco Studios night watchman thought he could smell smoke. He opened the door to stage number one only to find the set engulfed in flames. Before the fire brigade could get the blaze under control, the majority of the MacNeil house had burned to the ground, along with the numerous expensive antiques and paintings used to dress it. The cocooned version of Regan's bedroom remained untouched in studio number two, but still, the fire meant more weeks of delays and another major upswing in the budget as the set was rebuilt, now for the third time.

In between filming on the refrigerated bedroom set, Max von Sydow was being whisked away by Dick Smith to a hot room, with temperatures of up to 120 degrees. Here, Smith worked on perfecting the make-up von Sydow would wear in the forthcoming Iraq shoot, where the prologue to the film was due to be filmed. Smith's original make-up would not sustain the heat of that location so he was experimenting with a new form of waterproof latex. The almost hourly changes in climate for von Sydow resulted in the actor falling ill, once again causing delays and rescheduling in the filming. In addition to this, an unexpected problem with the refrigeration system positioned above Regan's bedroom led to a flash flood on the set, again necessitating several days of waiting for the principal set to dry out.

Despite such conditions and inevitable delays, Friedkin remained optimistic and adrenaline-charged throughout. The man who had prided himself on being able to shoot twenty-five to thirty-five set-ups a day on *The French Connection* was now down to only one or two per day, many of which would have to be redone when such variables as the piano wire being visible were revealed by the following day's rushes. "There was a degree of frustration," says Friedkin, "But I had an inherent belief in the film that transcended something as mundane as frustration."

Others were not so convinced: "I really don't know how much we went over schedule," recollects Dick Smith. "But it was considerable. It seemed like forever. I remember Ellen Burstyn came in one morning to the make-up room, when most of the actors were in there, and she said 'I had the most awful nightmare last night. I dreamt they told us that the series had been bought.' The nightmare was that this was not a film, but a TV series of like thirty episodes or something enormous and this had been bought for up to two or three years. It was never gonna end. That was her nightmare. We all groaned in sympathy."

One of the key scenes in both the novel and the film of *The Exorcist* is what has become known as the crucifix masturbation scene, a deeply disturbing and violently shocking moment when the possessed Regan plunges a metal and wood crucifix repeatedly into her vagina in the presence of her mother and the psychiatrist, imploring "Let Jesus fuck you." For Friedkin, it was the single defining image of his movie, something that in his mind put sex and religion in the same arena on screen: "The crucifix and vagina are things that never appear together. They're taboo in most people's consciousness. Yet I think they're very much related in the way that all things are related, but very specifically. I think a lot of religious belief comes from a kind of sexual hysteria as well. Not a specific act of sexuality but I think that the effect is not dissimilar in terms of what happens in religious passion and what happens in sexual passion. And yet they are never brought together in the same frame or the same room even, other than in a blasphemous way. In a way it was depicting blasphemy. And in a mainstream commercial movie you don't depict blasphemy. For many years you couldn't say Goddammit on the screen."

The scene required Linda Blair to sit astride a box, filled with fake red blood and positioned off screen, plunging the crucifix into the box between her legs. (Eileen Dietz's leg was briefly featured in another shot.) "I think the masturbation scene was one of the worst things I've ever had to do in my life," Blair explained to Kermode. "I didn't understand what masturbation was at that age. There was a box and a sponge with red food colouring. I just had to put the cross in the box – that's all I was doing. I'd no idea what it was until many years later. You just do what you're told to do and you're embarrassed."

"The thing with the crucifix," remembers Dick Smith "is that it was a problem which had to be referred to the so-called censor. What would, what wouldn't be allowed? And Billy Friedkin was told to his amusement, that the key was moderation, not excess. So if she [Blair] swung or wielded the crucifix one time that would be OK. I'd finished the film and six months later I was in Hollywood for something else and I called up Billy and he said 'Come over, I've just finished editing this scene.' So I came over and I sat alone in the screening room and of course, for every bit of film I'd been there on set, but here the scene came with such power in that one minute of screen time. I sat there and chills went up my spine. It just carried me away and I said 'My God, this is going to be a fantastic film.'"

In planning the scene, Friedkin was well aware of the potentially controversial nature of the image he was dealing with. While the attention was obviously focused on Regan, Friedkin pulled off something of a smoke and mirrors trick with the rest of the room. Recalling incidents the aunt of the possessed boy in the 1949 case had relayed to him, Friedkin decided to distract the audience's attention by having the room turn into a chaotic nightmare of flying, swirling objects. Marcel Vercoutere supplied the know-how. The effects man built two troughs – eighteen inches wide and six inches deep – into which he piped compressed air tanks. "They were about twenty-two to twenty-four hundred pounds per square inch. I piped indirectly, with quick-action valves, to the back of these troughs that I built. Then I aimed them both at the window. Now we could take anything we wanted to – books, records, dolls – and put then on the chutes. I had prop men standing by on both sides and just before Ellen Burstyn opened up the door, I hit these quick-action valves. And now you have an air stream that is just tremendous. And it flew straight, clean to the other end of the room, bounced off the walls, the windows, everything. We had dozens and dozens of things literally flying."

As laborious as the process of filming had become, Friedkin was determined to keep his cast as alert and responsive as possible and to these ends, he began to employ a number of unique – and not always welcome – devices.

"Billy had some idiosyncrasies," offers Dick Smith diplomatically. "But it was his perfectionism that drove him to try everything he could think of to try and make it better. For instance, if they were getting a close-up done on someone and the person they were supposed to be reacting to, namely Linda, could not be in front of him, Billy would have an African mask or something as a target. He would try to pick something horrible to make it easier for the actor to motivate or react, or whatever it is an actor does. And in the early scene where Regan grabs the psychiatrist by the balls, it said in the script that the demon manifests this horrible smell. Well, you can't show that in film but he wanted the actors to react to a real stench so Billy told the special effects guy: 'Cook me up something really nasty. I don't know what, old tennis shoes and limburger cheese or whatever.' And they came up with something and brought it on the set, and it truly was nauseous. Ellen Burstyn immediately covered her nose with her handkerchief and sent her wardrobe lady up to her room to get some perfume out of her purse to soak the handkerchief. And at one point she said to Billy: 'Billy, if I throw up, where do you want me to do it?' And Chris Newman, the soundman, cut right in and said 'Ellen, I don't care where you do it, just don't overlap a line.'"

At other times, Friedkin would keep his actors in the dark over the nature of approaching scenes, such as the time he left Max von Sydow unprepared for the torrent of obscenities spewing forth from the possessed Regan. "I insisted we rehearse every night," Jason Miller told The Fear Of God team. "And Linda might like to mouth the words. And I remember on the day when we had to film – and Max was very paternal to her, rubbed her head and talked to her – and she gets on this bed and Friedkin says 'Action!' And Linda looks up with her beautiful blue eyes and cherubic face and says 'Your mother sucks cocks in Hell.' And Max goes 'Cut! . . . I've lost it Billy, I've just lost it.' Of course we all lost it. Everybody lost it when you see that little girl say that line."

"I'll never forget that expression on his face," Friedkin said of von Sydow at the time. "When this man whose concentration is, bar none, the best, went right up when he heard the first obscenity, I knew that we must have a good film."

One of Friedkin's more extreme notions was to shoot off guns, strategically hidden on set, to provoke the desired startled response from his actors. "In the exorcism as that progressed, he used more and more gunshots until it was getting a little crazy," continues Smith. "But it must have worked because everyone certainly reacted. It back-fired a couple of times. There was one time when Karl the butler [Rudolph Schundler] was on the stairs and he was supposed to be suddenly startled and Billy shot off a gun and the poor man nearly fell down the stairs. He blew his lines completely because he was so startled."

Jason Miller for one was someone who didn't appreciate Friedkin's penchant for direction by .45. It was ostensibly a simple scene: Karras sits listening to the tape he has made of the demon/Regan when the phone rings, startling him. "That really pissed me off," continues Miller. "I told him, I said 'Never do that again. I'm an actor. I don't need these artificial stimulants.' I was in that room all alone, and my son was in the hospital and I was a little jumpy then. He was still in a coma. He had me sitting there and he had this absolute silence in the room and I'm listening to the tape and trying to decipher it when the phone rings. He wanted my reaction to the phone to create some kind of tension in the scene. So he and I did it a couple of times and on the third or fourth take the phone rings. I pick it up and ahhh! this shotgun goes off, this close to my head. I said 'You son of a bitch. How dare you do that? What if you went a little too far to the right?' And Friedkin said 'It's alright, we've got Jack Nicholson in the wings.' I had to laugh. It was a good line."

As director of photography, Owen Roizman recalls the cast soon took the firearms in their stride: "The actors would come in in the morning and like Max would say 'Good morning Owen, where are the guns today?' And I'd go 'Well there's a .45 behind that wall and a shotgun behind that wall. Thank you very much.' "

"He had total freedom," von Sydow explained to the BBC "And he behaved like a man with total freedom and total power. I enjoyed very much working with him although he sometimes used methods that I was not used to." (Von Sydow's patience would eventually be tested when the production relocated to Iraq and one week's shooting became several, with the actor ultimately forced to deliver an ultimatum to Friedkin informing him that he would stay for another four days and that was it.)

Friedkin defends all his actions, insisting that the end certainly did justify the means: "I shot blanks on the set a few times just to get the actors in a mood where they were all keyed up. And it works. It works every time you do that. They were cap pistols and it was a technique that was not invented by me. I read that George Stevens did that when he filmed *The Diary Of Anne Frank* to make the actors who were portraying the Frank family terrified on screen when they were supposed to be listening to the sirens of the German police cars. And of course when you're filming an actor's reaction to something when they're supposed to be terrified – say it's a police car – you don't often play the sound on the stage. They have to act it; they've got to fake it. One of the toughest things to fake is genuine fear. A lot of actors don't understand that. A lot of actors will say I don't need all those devices – I'm an actor, I can act it. And in every single case I always let the actor do it first without any supplemental device: 'OK, you're supposed to be afraid, you're seeing God knows what, a demon appear in a room or whatever, go ahead – Action!'. And it's generally shit, or unbelievable or over the top, because what directing is, for the most part, is providing an atmosphere in which this stuff can unfold. Sometimes it's an atmosphere of great tranquillity, other times it's chaos. If what you're trying to portray on the screen is chaos, as a director you generally have to create a chaotic environment to get the ultimate reaction to something like that. But you'll hear almost every actor, after the fact say: well, I don't need that shit, I'm an actor. But they don't know what they're doing, what effect they're producing in the way that a director knows and looks at and says I don't believe that. So you do it again and again."

One of the last scenes to be filmed was the possession of Karras. After several weeks of discussing this pivotal scene, which takes place 'off camera' as it were in Blatty's novel, it was Jason Miller who hit upon a solution. "One day I went in and I said 'Let me hit her, just punch the shit out of her.' That's evil" Miller recalled for the BBC. "We were running around for two weeks trying to define how you manifest evil in that scene and finally, out of my own frustration, I said 'let me take her off the bed and whack her' and he's gonna kill her and that means the devil is now in him. So we got a couple of dolls and we tried it, and you saw him become transformed because now the element of doubt has opened this chasm of vulnerability, the Devil sneaks in and now he's got him. And he's gonna kill this girl. It's homicidal rage coming out of him. And that's what we decided would be the ultimate action of that particular scene.

"I thought," the actor continues "What should happen to Karras was that his mother's face should have come right out in him, and that really would have shown the immense superior power of an evil force. I thought they would have gone for that. There would be almost a subliminal glimpse, but it would be his mother, and it would go right by his face. And that would be the devil toying with him and playing with him, and that would be one of the things he would certainly have to overcome by going out the window. But we reduced it to the green eyes [Dick Smith's contact lenses]. Again, just a subliminal thing."

After 224 days of principal photography – considerably more than the eighty-five days originally scheduled – filming of *The Exorcist* came to an end. For many, but not for all. With the logic common to all film productions, the last thing to be shot was, naturally, the beginning. In his first draft screenplay, Bill Blatty had omitted the prologue – set in Iraq – from his novel. Friedkin had wisely insisted on it being reinstated, providing the film with not only some of its most powerful images, but effectively establishing the character of Merrin (who subsequently remains off screen until the final act) and presaging the battle between good and evil that was to come.

For the majority of the film's shooting, Bill Blatty's battle had not been between good and evil, but between himself as Hollywood producer and the Iraqi government: "I was the one who arranged to get them into northern Iraq because I spoke Arabic. I went to the Iraqi embassy day after day romancing somebody in the consulate's office and showing him how I, an American, could speak Arabic. I don't think any company before or since has ever shot in Iraq. It took several months of negotiating. They were very suspicious. I'd been there when I was with the US Information Service. And I went up to central and northern Iraq to gather material for the magazine that we published. And the day I left, my train – the Orient Express – left at midnight, so I wandered about looking at this and that, and there was an archaeological dig and the sun was hitting it in just such a way and I thought 'Oh my God, some day I have to write about this.' And that's how the prologue came to be."

With the budget already well over its original predictions, Warners were keen to get the movie finished and tried to persuade Friedkin to relocate the Iraqi sequence to the nearby Mojave desert. "They didn't understand why I had to go to Iraq," the director says. "I thought it was necessary for the verisimilitude I was looking for. Of course I had never been to Iraq prior to that, only had still photographs of it. What I learned was at the time the United States government had no diplomatic relations with Iraq. After months along came the reluctant permission to go there at which point I said

'Jesus Christ, this could be life threatening and dangerous, and I don't know what I'm going to find and I don't know if they'll let me do it.' Again, my direction of *The Exorcist* was pretty much a leap into the void on all cylinders."

The Exorcist became the first Western movie to receive permission to film in the Iraqi desert, at the towns of Mosul and Hatra, where the excavation site where we first encounter Merrin was located. Max von Sydow was the only principal cast member required. Accompanying Friedkin was a small crew that included make-up man Dick Smith, first assistant director Terrence Donnelly, set designer Bill Malley, sound man Jean Louis Ducarne (brought in from Paris) and, from London, gaffer Jimmy Harris. Smith brought along Rick Baker to assist him on von Sydow's three-hour make-up. Cameraman Billy Williams replaced Owen Roizman as the director of photography for this section of the movie. (Roizman was exhausted from the main shoot having been diagnosed as diabetic when filming first began.)

The crew met up with the actor in Baghdad and were all set to travel the 310 kilometres north to their first location at Mosul, when Donnelly noticed they were one short. The one in question was the six foot statue of the demon Pazuzu (the personification of the south-west wind whose dominion was sickness and disease). This all-powerful ancient god had apparently fallen victim to incompetent baggage handlers: "A great panic occurred – 'where the hell is Pazuzu?' " laughs Dick Smith. "Finally, it appeared in Hong Kong. They never took it off the plane. How could they miss this Goddamn monstrosity of a thing?"

Friedkin was immediately enchanted with the beauty of the Iraqi desert and filmed well over three hours of material for his ten-minute opening prologue. Various other problems – Bill Malley came down with dysentery, Jimmy Harris dropped a heavy object on his foot and severed a toe – and the heat, which necessitated the crew filming from 6 a.m. to 11 a.m., then breaking until late afternoon – meant that what had originally been scheduled as a one-week shoot soon grew to nearly six weeks. Because of the nature of his make-up, Max von

Sydow, along with Smith and Baker, began their day at 2 a.m.

The crew filmed for several days in Mosul, where they stayed at the Railroad Station Hotel (located not surprisingly by the local railway station) before journeying further afield to Hatra. Along the way, Friedkin took time to meet with, and photograph, a tribe of devil worshippers, who he described as being "reminiscent of the Charley Manson mob" who, amongst other practices, refused to eat lettuce or cabbage, believing the Devil lived in those foods.

Footage was being shipped to Baghdad and then on to London, but several reels of film from the first few days of shooting were lost, forcing production manager Bill Kaplan to spend several days tracking them down all over Iraq. Two of them had made their way to London without the proper clearance; another two were found sitting out in the sun at the Mosul depot. From then on it was decided not to ship the film out for processing, meaning that Friedkin had no way to check on what he was filming until he returned to New York.

Hatra provided the film with the excavation site – a partially unearthed Assyrian bathhouse. It was also the place where the now located and delivered Pazuzu came into its own: "Billy went out to scout and find a proper location for Pazuzu," says Smith. "So he finds this small hill for it, because in the film Pazuzu is supposed to be on one hill and Max von Sydow comes up on the other hill and confronts it. Billy then decided that it would be a real ominous pictorial thing to have a couple of hawks flying in the sky overhead. So he sends to England and they bring down four hawks and two trainers, only to discover when they get to Baghdad that hawks do not fly in 120 degree temperatures. So they all had to go back to England. Not giving up, someone suggests 'Why don't we get some vultures? They have vultures down here. They must fly.' So someone is sent over to the native village of sheep herders, and he buys a slaughtered lamb, and he brings it back and he places it by the statue. A couple of days pass and there's not a damn vulture in sight. And this guy has to go back to the village for something else and he comes back laughing and says 'Do you know what they're saying in the village? They said this strange man has come from America and he's offering sacrifices to Pazuzu.' That was the Arab viewpoint on what us mad Americans were doing."

Dick Smith had expressed his concerns to Friedkin over travelling to such a politically volatile country. His fears were realised when the Iraqi chief of police Nassim Kazar attempted to stage a coup d'état, the very day the film crew travelled to Hatra. President Ahmed Hassan Al-Bakr was in Poland on diplomatic business. Friedkin described the incident to journalist Peter Travers, calling it the greatest adventure of his life: "The plan was to take a squad of men to the airport to kill the President when his plane landed from Poland. Prior to this action they had kidnapped and killed ministers in the government. But the President's plane was delayed for two hours. During this time lapse, the conspirators panicked and failed. There were forty people rounded up, including the chief of police, and they were charged with complicity. The President inpanelled a three-judge committee for a trial and the next day twenty-six were hanged, and the day after that, thirteen more. Justice is pretty swift over there. The man who engineered this plot had allegedly made a gentleman's agreement with one of Iraq's greatest competitors. So, if this plan had worked, the effects internationally would have been unbelievable. This political intrigue happened two miles from where we were staying, so in a manner of speaking we were prisoners."

The Iraqi airline that had misplaced the statue of Pazuzu were also responsible for the delay in the arrival of the President's plane, leaving Kazar's attempt to usurp the country as probably the only political coup in history that was averted due to a dodgy airline. "We didn't know about it of course until the next morning," says Smith. "I said 'Billy, if that had succeeded, what would we have done?' We were out in the middle of nowhere and he said, 'Well, the only thing we could have done was pile into all our vehicles and head for the nearest border as fast as we could.' My fears were almost realised. Thank God they weren't.'"

One of the two films that Friedkin admits to having influenced him was Stanley Kubrick's *2001 – A Space Odyssey* (the other is Orson Welles' *Citizen Kane*, which of course had set him on the path to filmmaking after he had seen it at the Surf Theatre all those years before). Within *The Exorcist* he wanted to place a talisman – something that would move between location and character, unifying these people in a transcendent manner. He chose as this symbol a Christian medallion of St Joseph, first discovered by Father Merrin alongside a small amulet of Pazuzu in the archaeological dig, later seen being worn by Father Karras, ripped from Karras's neck by Regan during the final exorcism and, finally, handed back to Father Dyer as a remembrance of his dead friend by Chris MacNeil as she and Regan prepare to leave Georgetown.

"I was looking for something akin to the obelisk in *2001*," Friedkin admits. "Something from another time and place that keeps appearing in different guises. That's not from the novel. Something that would transcend time and space and place, and was a kind of talisman that gave the film a sort of unity across many continents and across many different periods of time because I felt this work could be looked at as a kind of prophecy with a timeless quality. A quality of not only the mystery of faith but the mystery of fate. How fate unites people from disparate worlds, brings them together over a highly charged dramatic event that ultimately affects all of their lives, even though they're all brought together from various persuasions, various countries, various points of view, whatever. And I felt that the St Joseph's medal could serve that purpose. I was thinking: what if something that could be found in Iraq could wind up on Father Karras's neck, be pulled off him by Regan while she's possessed, ultimately be handed over to Chris MacNeil at the end of the film, and she then gives it back to Father Karras's friend, Father Dyer, which again strengthens this notion of a continuity of events that had affected all these peoples' lives. For a movie it was a rather mystical idea, not unlike the way Kubrick used the obelisk. And the way *Citizen Kane* used the Rosebud sled. I'm very conscious that all of this stuff is in one way or another influenced by something else. One thing leads to another. And in the seventies with almost everything I did I was referencing *Citizen Kane* or *2001*, which are clearly the two most influential films in my life."

When Bill Blatty saw the Iraq footage he was less than happy with Friedkin's talisman: "I have never liked that," he still maintains. "When Billy came back I saw that footage. I said: 'Bill what is a St Joseph's medal with Latin written on it doing in a 3,000-year-old archaeological site?' And Billy said 'Resonance.' And he turned on his heel and walked away. Now here's the curious thing – I remember one review of the film in which the reviewer said 'Well, this is preposterous. Can you believe Lt Kinderman finds a piece of the statue of the demon Pazuzu at the foot of those steps in Georgetown?' Well, of course it was just a piece of the little sculpture that Regan had made and knocked off the window ledge when she pushed Burke Dennings out. So they jumped all over that, but not this critic or any other critic in the entire universe ever said 'What is a St Joseph's medal doing in an archaeological dig in northern Iraq?' It doesn't make any sense, but nobody ever noticed. Once you do a motion picture with a supernatural background and supernatural events occur, you might be able to expect something like a St Joseph's medal. But what I do not expect is for a noted palaeontologist- archaeologist like Father Merrin in looking at the medal to say 'This is strange, not of the same period.'"

As the crew prepared to leave Iraq, some of the local tribesmen, who had worked as extras, decided to throw a small party for them in one of their mud huts. This became an impromptu birthday party for sound man Jean Louis Ducarne, where the locals were greatly taken by the notion of a cake with candles on it.

Back in New York, Friedkin completed the remaining shots for Karras's dream sequence, an extended nightmare that links images from Iraq – the stopped clock, the savage dogs, the St Joseph's medallion – with Karras on the streets of New York, calling out to his mother who he sees in the distance descending into the subway, a N.Y. stand-in for Hell.

And then, the filming of *The Exorcist* was complete.

THE DEVIL HAS ALL THE BEST TUNES

While the power of having the pre-pubescent Linda Blair deliver such lines as "Stick your cock up her ass, you motherfucking, worthless cocksucker" (to give but one example), was undeniable, Friedkin knew that Blair's voice would not be strong enough on its own to portray the full ferocity of the demon. Throughout production he had experimented with various means of capturing the right voice. Initially he contacted Ken Nordine, an old colleague from his TV days in Chicago, who had worked with the director on the Chicago Symphony Orchestra broadcasts.

"He's a brilliant guy with voices and stuff," says Friedkin. "He's made a fortune doing commercials but to a great extent they're all experimental sound commercials and he actually released several record albums that were, in their own way, quite successful called *Word Jazz*. And I sent him Linda Blair's tracks, recorded on the set, and he had discussed several approaches he was going to take experimentally. He then sent me back some of his experiments. And he'd weirded out the voice or distorted it or stuff like that, but it all sounded like Ken Nordine. It all sounded like this great baritone voice of a distinguished guy. Wrong. You'd look at it and say: 'This is Linda Blair? No way.' Then I'd sit down and think: well, what is right? If this is wrong, what's right?"

In thinking it through, Friedkin decided that the voice must be in keeping with the realistic approach of the rest of his movie and must therefore by default be a neutral voice, one that could encompass a young girl and an ancient demon. But who had such a neutral voice? Friedkin quickly remembered the actress Mercedes McCambridge, veteran of such movies as Orson Welles' *Touch Of Evil*, and a Best Supporting Actress Oscar winner for *All The King's Men*.

"The name just came into my mind, like the movie god. I had no idea if she was still alive, but I remembered her from dramatic radio which used to be a staple of American life. Radio drama was a very important part of American cultural life when I grew up. I was very influenced by radio drama, and one of the great voices on radio drama was Mercedes McCambridge. Terrific actress, great voice. I asked my production manager to find out where the hell she was and if she was still alive. Yes, she was still alive, in fact she was working somewhere in Texas on stage doing *Who's Afraid Of Virginia Wolf?* We got her phone number. I called her and told her what was going on. She was fascinated by it and said 'I've got three weeks until I finish this play, then I'll come to Hollywood and we'll talk.' She came in after she finished the play. I ran the movie for her, she was very moved by it and she said 'Yes, I think I can do this.' So I then entered into an agreement with her to use her as the demon voice, of course with distortions and other things that I added to the voice. But essentially it's her performance."

"William Friedkin called me and he said he had a special interest in having me do a one hundred per cent radio performance in a film," Ms McCambridge told the BBC in 1998. "And he asked me if I had read *The Exorcist*, and I said I tried to read it on an aeroplane and I threw it across the room. But he said 'I want you to read it and I want you to come to New York. . . . I'm in the editing room now. I have the film, it's all finished and I'd like to show it to you. So I stopped on my way in Washington to see a priest and I said 'Father, he wants me to play the Devil. What if I get possessed or something?' And he said 'My dear girl, you are an actress. If you took on everything that you played, you would be an inmate, not an actress.' "

Having viewed the film in New York, McCambridge decided she

wanted to play the role of the Devil, and relocated to the Warner Brothers lot in Hollywood to record the part, which took Friedkin a total of three weeks to stage and record, with the actress going to great lengths to achieve the desired effects.

"Linda Blair vomited pea soup," McCambridge said. "I thought, how am I going to make that sound? Well, we went over to the commissary at Warner Brothers and we got a big bowl – and we did this every morning because it took several days to get that sound – and we would take apples and cut them up into tiny little pieces, and they would soften in warm water so that they would just be bumps. Then we'd get a dozen eggs each day and we'd get cups, and we'd put two eggs into six cups and they'd line those up in front of me, along with six microphones. And they had to cover the microphones with scrim so I wouldn't get all that stuff on them. I would put the little pieces of apple in my mouth and then I would take two of the eggs, not mixed up or anything, just the yolk and the white part, and put those in my mouth and swallow all of it, and then at exactly the right second, I would hit it and vomit it on to the microphone. And I would be watching the screen to synchronise with Linda Blair throwing up the pea soup vomit. I had to synchronise that with the stuff that came out of my mouth."

On another occasion the actress was tied to a chair. "I didn't think they had to do this, but they did. They tore up a sheet and put me in restraints, around my neck and my arms behind the chair, and my knees and feet so that I would feel like Linda Blair while she was carrying on in the bed. I would be doing the same thing physically."

"Some of the stuff was my idea, some of it was hers," Friedkin explains. "She had two parish priests there at all times for counselling and guidance while we recorded this. One of the things that she felt she needed to do to get her voice into a certain range and tone was to start drinking again. She was a reformed alcoholic and she said 'I know how my voice sounds when I'm drinking, and I'll do that but it's got to be under controlled conditions with my priests there.' So we did that and some of it was very physically difficult for her. And we did it line by line, trial and error, take after take.

Sometimes I would combine two takes in one, using one track playing over another very often. But it was a rather lengthy process and it worked pretty well."

"Doing the soundtrack was a terrible experience," McCambridge told the *New York Times*. "I didn't just do the voice – I did all the demon's sounds. That wheezing, for instance. My chronic bronchitis helped with that. I did it on one microphone, then on another, elevating it a bit, then a third and fourth, two tones higher each time, and they combined them as a chorus. The wailing just before the demon is driven out – that's the keening sounds I once heard at a wake in Ireland. I used moaning cries I had used when playing Lady Macbeth for Orson [Welles]. For the groaning sounds, I pulled a scarf around my neck tight and almost strangled."

So impressive was Mercedes McCambridge's demonic performance in the final film that Friedkin contrived to keep the origin of the Devil a secret, denying McCambridge a previously agreed to on screen credit.

"There was a sneak preview at the Westwood Theatre in Westwood," the actress recalled to Mark Kermode. "And I knew that Warner Brothers and Billy Friedkin would be there. This was the first preview. So I thought, I wonder if there's a way of sneaking into the back of the theatre? And I'm sitting there on the side, slumped way down so that I could get to see the movie but they wouldn't know I was there. So I saw it and oh, my good Lord it was a spectacular display – the whole thing. And now the movie's over and the credits are being run. And the furrier got a credit, everybody in the whole world got a credit. And then the screen went to black. Where was mine? So I started out of the theatre. I was really so upset. I was crying and Billy saw me and he started chasing me out into the parking lot. And I saw a mustang. I had a mustang and it was valet parking and the keys were in it, but it wasn't my car. I drove it three blocks before I realised I had a stolen car here. But I was hysterical at the time and when I came back to the parking lot they had all left."

McCambridge's undeniable contribution to the movie was later championed by the New York Times and her name was instated on the credits of all bar the first thirty or so prints of the movie.

(When the movie was sold to CBS Television in the eighties, Friedkin chose to redub the demon voice himself rather than work with McCambridge again. "All of the obvious dialogue had to be changed. So we had to loop lines like 'Your mother sucks cocks in Hell', which in the TV version now says 'Your mother still rots in Hell.' I wasn't too anxious to work with McCambridge anymore. She was a pain in the ass and she wanted a lot of money to do it, and the studio turned to me with their hands up and said 'What else are we gonna do?' So I said 'Let me have a crack at it. I think I know how to achieve this now, and I think I can mimic it.' So it's my voice on the television version, which is the worst version of the picture." Friedkin also re-filmed one scene for this TV version – the desecrated statue of Mary, which now features lipstick and eye shadow, as opposed to the phallus seen in the theatrical release.)

Bernard Herrman was Billy Friedkin's first choice to score his movie. Herrman's distinctive film soundtrack career had included such classics as the inevitable *Citizen Kane* and the brilliantly inventive score for Alfred Hitchcock's *Psycho*. Eager to have his movie stand alongside those renowned works, Friedkin sought out Herrman who was at the time based in London.

"He was hands down the greatest composer of American film music," enthuses the director. *"Citizen Kane, Psycho, The Birds, The Magnificent Ambersons, The Devil & Daniel Webster* – a masterful composer. He was very angry at America and had moved to England, and was doing a little bit of film work, not a lot. I sent him the film and then I went over to England to meet with him. And by this time he was a crotchety old guy. He had made some recordings at a church called St Giles, where he loved the sound of the church organ. I met him after he had screened the film at William Morris in London. We met there and he said 'Well, it's an interesting film but you've got to take out the first ten minutes of it – all that bullshit in Iraq. That gets you nowhere. It has nothing to do with any of the rest of the story; it's just fucking boring. Get rid of that shit, a few other things and I think my music can probably save it.' I said 'OK.' And he said 'Of course I gotta record it here. I ain't going to America. I fucking hate Hollywood, it's better here and it's cheaper, and I've got this church where I have this great organ.' I was really awed by the guy, but now he's talking and he said 'organ' and I said 'Do you really think a church organ is appropriate? Don't you think it's a bit clichéd for this film?' He said 'No, no, no kid. You don't know what I'm gonna do with an organ. It's not gonna sound like the Mormon Tabernacle choir or High Church. I'm gonna use an organ the way I use an organ.' I said 'But it's still going to be an organ in a church.' He said 'Leave that to me.' I said 'Well, OK. I'd like to be here while you record.' He said 'Be here? Are you kidding me? When I get done with my score, I'll mail you the tracks.' And I looked at him and I shook his hand, and I said 'Thank you for letting me meet an interesting person' and that was it – no way. I had come too far with the film even to give it to the man who I thought was the very best. I didn't feel comfortable with his approach."

Billy had met Lalo Schifrin back in his Chicago days, when the young Argentinean pianist had sat in on several occasions with the Dizzy Gillespie Quartet. Friedkin, a big jazz fan at the time, often used to see the Quintet and got to know Schifrin. Lalo had ambitions to write film music; Billy wanted to make movies. Several years later the former had composed such successful works as the classic theme to TV's *Mission: Impossible* and the latter had made *The French Connection*. It was a natural, hometown connection that drew Friedkin to commission Schifrin to score *The Exorcist* after parting ways with Bernard Herrman.

"Lalo Schifrin was scheduled to record for a week, I think," Friedkin remembers. "Of course all of his scores were Latin influenced. So when I went to him to do the score for *The Exorcist*, I said to him 'Lalo, this cannot be a samba score. It can't be rhythmic. I don't want it to sound like music. I want it to be more tonal and moody. I want the music to be, in effect, a cold hand on the back of your neck. Nothing that you can put your finger on. Almost monolithic and sterile. Not emotional.' I said 'I don't really think we need to drive the audience's emotions with this score, but simply to enhance the moods on the screen subtly.' And I brought him some examples of contemporary classical music that I had been listening to – George Crumb, Krzysztof Penderecki and Anton Webern, in particular. We listened to these examples and he went out and wrote his music and played me some on the piano. It sounded OK, I guess. To my amazement I showed up at the recording session at Warner Brothers and there were ninety or one hundred musicians. And all the examples of the music that I played for him were chamber music. There's ninety or one hundred musicians; there's three or four percussionists alone – what the hell is this? Then he started playing. He went into the first cue and it was loud, bombastic, hammering, percussive. And I was in the control room and I couldn't believe it. I didn't say anything. The next couple of cues went along. It was the same thing – noisy and bombastic. I finally went out to him at the podium and said 'Lalo, I don't get this stuff. It's not what we talked about.' He said 'What's wrong with it?' I said 'First of all, it's too loud; it's too noisy.' So we went into the control room, played it – it's loud, noisy, bombastic. He went over to the master volume and he just turned the volume down. So it was a hundred guys playing loud with the volume turned down. That's all. I said 'No, no, that's not what I mean. This is characteristically wrong.' And he said 'Well, let me record a few more cues. If you continue to think that way then we have a real problem and I'll stop and I'll talk.' He went out and recorded a few more cues. I felt the same, then we sat down to talk and I said 'This is not what I'm looking for; it's not what we talked about. Can you change it?' And he said 'No, I can't. This is my score.' And I said 'That's it. It's over.' "

Friedkin was allegedly so displeased with Schifrin's score that when one of his sound editors attempted to mix some innocuous part of it under the scene of Chris MacNeil's Washington cocktail party, the director took the reel of tape and threw it outside into the middle of the street claiming that was where Schifrin's score belonged.

Unable to find a composer who could deliver what he wanted, Friedkin went back to the sources he had been playing for inspiration, incorporating classical works by Penderecki, Webern, Crump, David Borden and Hans Werner Henze into his score.

However, there was one key element of the score that he still had to find: "I was looking for something that would be kind of a nursery rhyme motif and I spoke to the head of Warner Music at that time – a guy named Larry Marks, whom I had great communication with. I told him what I was looking for, but I couldn't define it too well. He said 'Well, in my office there's a whole bunch of stuff that no one's ever heard from companies that we own and they're sending us demos to see if we want to release them. Go in and see if there's anything you like.' I went in and I picked out all these LPs and I started putting a needle to them and I'd listen to four bars and go 'Next, next, next.' I don't know how long it was before I heard this thing called *Tubular Bells* by Mike Oldfield. It was sent in to Warner Brothers to see if they wanted to release it in America. I don't believe they were going to. I listened to it and that motif of *Tubular Bells* was exactly what I was looking for. Immediately after that motif appears, you then hear the voice of Mike Oldfield doing a narration, talking about the meaning of the sound of bells, whatever – I don't know. It's very boring, but that motif struck me as being exactly what I was looking for. So we easily retained the rights to it and I put it in the film. And I think they sold a million records of it as a result. In his autobiography Richard Branson says it's the single piece of music that made his company, Virgin. I've never met Richard Branson or spoken to him to this day. Or Mike Oldfield."

"When I'm shooting I want to get it all on film," Friedkin has said. "Everything that I can possibly think about a scene. I say 'Let's film.' But when I'm editing, I'm ruthless. I sit down and curse the actor's images on the movieola, the lighting, the composition. I rip it apart. I'm like a third party. I come in with an attitude like 'What is this piece of shit?' And that's how I edit the picture, with that attitude in mind."

Friedkin put his movie together in an editing studio, located appropriately at 666 Fifth Avenue in New York, with four teams of editors working simultaneously, headed by Bud Smith. The film not only needed to be ready for his scheduled release date of 26

December 1973 (to capitalise on the Christmas box office period and also to qualify for the Academy Awards, which require a film to have played to a public audience before the end of the previous year). It also had to be ready in time to face any problems that might arrive for its certification from the Motion Picture Association of America (MPAA). *The Exorcist* had to have an 'R' rating. An 'X' would diminish its audience and severely harm its chances at the box office. Friedkin had thirty hours of footage; he needed to produce a two-hour movie.

Friedkin, who thrives on the editing process and the controlled environment that allows him to finally bring together all the disparate elements and shape the film he had already seen in his mind, spoke openly to journalist Peter Travers during this time: "I like quickness on the screen. I like things to happen fast. It is my feeling that the audience today is two steps ahead of most filmmakers. So what I try to do in the cutting room is play a little game with that intelligent audience I have in my head. I look at the film and see, as usual, that we're going along A-B-C-D. But the audience, given A, is already at D. So I say, let's go right to D. If we're wrong, at least we won't be boring anybody.

"In *The Exorcist*," Friedkin continued "There is a combination of light and dark elements within each frame and from scene to scene to subtly suggest the struggle between good and evil. It's something I hope no critic will pick up on, because it's a technique that becomes simplistic when you put it into words – light and dark equals good and evil – and yet that's what I'm doing. I think of the images as a kind of dialogue between myself and the audience. But I put all of this behind telling the story. That's my primary interest and responsibility."

On 21 June 1973 Friedkin found himself face to face with a new obstacle. The Supreme Court passed a new piece of legislation effectively allowing local communities to rule on what they considered to be obscene. "I am concerned but not afraid," said Friedkin as he continued to edit his controversial movie. "It is a rough law. It threatens the entire film industry because it blurs the distinction between garbage and legitimate expression and makes every garden club in every small town a censor for movies. *The Exorcist* is not an obscene film or a dirty film. I'm not going to pretend it is. But it deals in highly controversial areas and as such, I realise it could run into trouble. I'm not going to run around cutting out allegedly controversial scenes. All the language and action depicted in this film have a foundation in the Catholic religion, in that they are all actual symptoms of possession. If *The Exorcist* gets banned, it will be because of the overall thrust of the film. I guarantee no one will say 'Take this scene out or take that scene out and it will be OK.' If *The Exorcist* isn't OK, it won't be OK from start to finish, not just a scene or two."

As he continued to edit his movie with this unexpected spectre hanging over him, Billy Friedkin read a resolution from the Directors' Guild of America into the Congressional Record vehemently opposing this new ruling. He concluded by saying: "Is it the intention of this provision to prosecute Stanley Kubrick for *A Clockwork Orange*, John Boorman and James Dickey for the book and film *Deliverance*, Bernardo Bertolucci and Marlon Brando for *Last Tango In Paris*, Henry Miller for *Tropic of Cancer*? Because if it is so intended, then the jails of this country are going to wind up with a larger talent roster than MGM had in the forties."

Friedkin screened his first cut of the movie for Bill Blatty in late September 1973. "Blatty was always my first audience for this movie. It was him I had to please first and foremost." The cut Friedkin showed the author and producer contained several scenes that would subsequently be excised. Blatty claims it was roughly twenty minutes longer; Friedkin maintains it was no more than seven or eight minutes, tops. Says Blatty now: "The film today is considered a classic; the film I saw on the movieola that day in New York at 666 Fifth Avenue was a masterpiece. That's the difference."

IN THE BLINK OF AN EYE –
SUBLIMINAL AND MAJOR CUTS

In a lecture-discussion conducted at the University of Georgia's film department shortly after the release of *The Exorcist*, William Friedkin stated: "The subliminal cut is the most important discovery the motion picture has made, in my opinion, since the close-up. And much more important than the dissolve or other discoveries that came after, that became part of the story-telling process on film. The subliminal cut is the single most provocative and useful tool that a filmmaker has today as a story-telling device because it really expresses the way all of us think in cinematic terms."

Picked up on this statement in 1998, Billy was rather less emphatic. "That's an outrageous phrase," he freely admits. "But the use of subliminal perception was not widely used at the time. There were only a couple of films I was aware of that had used it well. The first one of which was Alain Resnais's documentary *Night And Fog*, another one being Sidney Lumet's *The Pawnbroker*. But it occurred to me that subliminal perceptions were a powerful tool for this kind of thing if used sparingly. And so I employed it. It's clearly still a relatively unexplored area of contemporary filmmaking."

Greatly impressed and influenced by Resnais's documentary, which intercuts brief black-and-white shots of the bodies from a Jewish concentration camp into a colour tracking shot along the

Dick Smith's Regan Dummy

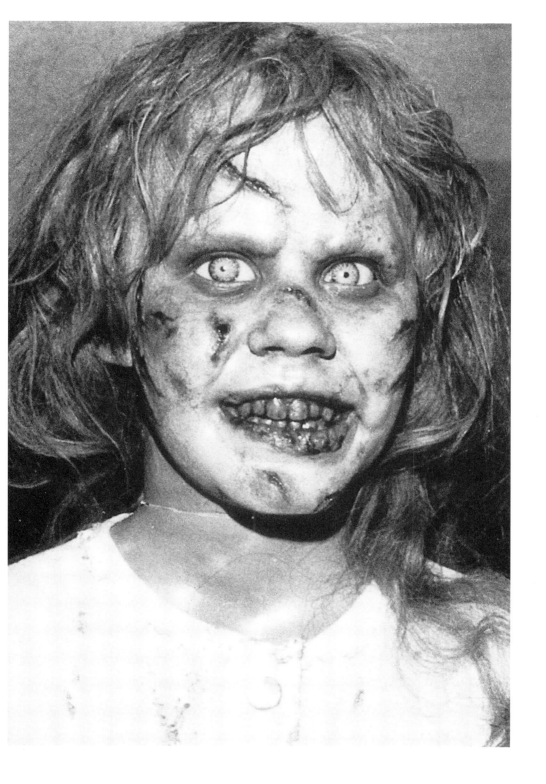

route into the camp today, now overgrown with wild grass and flowers, Friedkin decided to experiment with the use of the subliminal in his movie. As the movie became a phenomenon some would attempt to explain its power by use of these shots, greatly exaggerating both their amount and their impact in the film. The most obvious use of subliminal cuts occurs in the construction of Karras's dream. In 1991, Friedkin explained to *Video Watchdog* magazine the desired effect of this scene: "The pacing created by mixing shots that stay on the screen a little bit longer, with shots that stay on the screen for only a few frames, was kind of the way I perceived my own dreams."

More famous, and more contentious however, is the appearance of a ghost-like figure that first flashes through this dream sequence. Often referred to by *Exorcist* scholars as 'Captain Howdy', after Regan's 'imaginary' friend, this image is in fact a shot of Blair's double Eileen Dietz, modelling one of Dick Smith's early, and abandoned make-up design tests. This image later reoccurs twice during the final exorcism, once immediately after Regan's bed has levitated, and one final time during the second rotation of the dummy's head. This particular shot was actually an overlapping of two images, filmed on set, with Dick Smith making Dietz up in the ghost-like make-up. Optical effects expert Linwood Dunn used a beam-splitter to match a glass reflection of Dietz over a head shot of the dummy.

Friedkin of course also experimented with the use of subliminal sound in a number of ways in his movie, from blending the hammer and anvil banging of the workers in Iraq with the clatter of the New York subway train, to more extreme examples such as incorporating recordings of animals being slaughtered into the guttural sounds of Mercedes McCambridge. The overall effect on both audience and critics alike was even more powerful than Friedkin expected, leading to years of debate as to whether certain individual frames contained drawn-on images of ghostly faces appearing in the condensed breath of Father Merrin, and skull shadows appearing on the church wall behind Karras. The critic Wilson Bryan Hey can lay claim to many of these suppositions through his work *Media Sexploitation* which, amongst other things, incorrectly identified the shots of Eileen Dietz as a death-mask image of Karras, presumably presaging his demise.

The subliminal cuts debate rapidly became part of the legend that grew up around *The Exorcist*, as did the numerous scenes that were cut from the finished film, the most famous of which was the sequence referred to as the spider walk. This occurred both in the novel and the shooting script of the film, at the point immediately after Chris hears about the death of Burke Dennings. Regan then moves down the stairs, bent over backwards and walking on all fours like an insect. When she reaches the foot of the stairs, she turns, flicks out her long tongue and proceeds to chase Sharon (Kitty Winn). Marcel Vercoutere handled the technical side: "I made this rig that was in exactly the same position as the angle of the stairs" He explained to the *Fear Of God* team. Then I put a carriage up there, and then once I got her in the rig with the flying wires she stayed perfectly level, and all she had to do was let me know where her hand and feet would touch the steps. And then when she reached the landing, she turned over and I let her loose. It worked so well. I thought it added to the film because it was really frightening."

Friedkin was less convinced: "I just didn't think it worked for a lot of different reasons. One, it was one more visual effect that we didn't need, one that really stretched credulity. For example, why is she walking like a spider? In all of the other scenes Regan is basically victim of the attack by the demon. In that scene she is flaunting her demon-ness and I thought we were dealing with a story here that was stretching credulity enough at every turn. Why ask for more?"

The spider-walk was dropped early on from Friedkin's cut of the movie, as was a series of scenes shot around Washington as part of Regan's birthday sight-seeing trip, which amounted to little more than travelogue, although Blatty's script did include a dialogue between Chris and Regan at this point, where the child quizzes her mother on why people have to die, that Friedkin is believed to have shot. An earlier hospital visit for Regan was also filmed and dropped, primarily for pacing, leading to some mild confusion as, after

THE EXORCIST **Out of the Shadows**

urinating during the party episode, Regan asks her mother what's wrong with her. "It's just like the doctor says," Chris replies ". . . you just take your pills and you'll be fine. . . ." Any such doctorly advice was now missing from the film. "That's the very first major hole," Blatty told Video Watchdog in 1991. "It's like 'What's the matter honey? Gotta keep taking those pills.' What pills? When did she get sick? The last time I saw her, a minute ago, she was giggling and smiling downstairs."

Two other key scenes were included in the first cut that Friedkin showed to Blatty and the director's eventual decision to remove them led to a falling-out between the two men, which saw producer Blatty all but barred from the editing process hereafter.

"He was barred from the set because he was being a pain in the ass," Friedkin explained to *Video Watchdog*. "But my feeling is the great achievement of *The Exorcist* is his. It's his creation, his vision, his work. . . . In 99 per cent of the areas that were important, Blatty and I were in complete agreement. In 1 per cent we were not and it just so happened that I prevailed in that. But he prevailed in getting his vision on the screen. And it is his vision, not my own."

The first, and least significant, of these contentious scenes was the original ending to the novel in which Kinderman arrived and walked off into the distance talking to Father Dyer and quoting from the end scene of *Casablanca*. Friedkin originally cut this scene on the advice of Warner heads John Calley and Ted Ashley. "The studio's suggestion was that it was anticlimactic," Friedkin said at the time. "The minute I heard the suggestion I absolutely agreed with it."

"Bill Friedkin didn't want the movie to be too up and Bill Blatty wanted it to be resurrectional," Father William O'Malley told Mark Kermode. "The priest is dead, but the priest goes on. And Kinderman had found a friend, a priest again. In the beginning, I thought, who am I to criticise? But it was kinda nice to have the very last scene in a great big movie be nothing but *moi* all alone in the frame."

"I thought it was a lame way to end this movie," Friedkin still thinks today. "It's the ending in the book and it's very good, but the whole scene was nothing but a pastiche on the last scene of

Casablanca. I filmed it and I cut it. But I said 'Bill, why do we want to end our movie like *Casablanca*, using the dialogue of *Casablanca*? This is an original movie. Why hang that reference out there like that?' He liked it and he disagreed, and I ultimately prevailed, I think, for the good of the film because the film would have been seven or eight minutes longer. As it is, it's over two hours. It would be considered slow by today's standards at its two hours length. And it needed no more. But anyway, Bill didn't agree."

If Blatty didn't agree, he could at least forgive. He was less forgiving when it came to what for him was the pivotal scene of both the book and the film – the moment on the stairs during the exorcism, when Merrin explains to Karras that the Devil isn't after the child, it's after the observers, to make them doubt their faith. Blatty's argument (expressed much more eloquently than I have just here) was, for the author, the crystallisation of the theological debate of the whole story. It was shot, included in Friedkin's first cut, then dropped.

"Some of the scenes, I felt, were simply overstated and preachy when I looked at them, specifically the scene where Father Merrin tells Father Karras what this all means. There were other scenes where Blatty had the characters telling each other what the meaning was. And it seemed to me when I made the film, that the meaning was inherent in every frame. I didn't want some guy explaining it in the picture to some other character in the film and ultimately to the audience. I felt it needed no explanation. Like magic realism – there it is."

Jason Miller was another one who felt that by removing the majority of the dialogue between Merrin and Karras (a brief moment remains of them still sitting on the stairs), part of the film's spiritual meaning was lost: "Bill Friedkin was a filmmaker who said silence was more powerful than any kind of articulation of what was going on in their minds," the actor explained to the BBC. "I think we needed the articulation. Friedkin thought that silence was most eloquent there and that's what conveyed the most – these two men sitting on the steps with the stair poles between them. And Blatty felt that this is a time that Karras should articulate for the last time his real doubt about the efficacy of God and the supremacy of evil. And I agreed with Blatty. I think it was a crucial cut. It wasn't fatal, it certainly didn't hurt the film, but I think it would have added just one more thing. I think what Karras was doing was articulating what the audience was thinking in their heads."

Blatty's concern was that the audience would miss the point that Karras takes the demon into himself and then throws himself out of the window as an act of self-sacrifice and is not hurled to his death by the being within, something that many members of the audience did indeed misconstrue.

"Billy and I rehearsed every move of that ending because we were well aware that it could be misinterpreted," Blatty says "And we rehearsed everything that was going to happen so that it could not possibly be misinterpreted. And if you look at the scene over and over again, there's no question of what's really happening. But it's been so widely misinterpreted anyway. And I think the reason is that at that point in the film – especially if you're seeing it for the first time – you're numb with shock, you're not registering everything that's happening on that screen. I don't know what else can be done to get the real meaning at the end except for me to walk on stage with a card."

In early 1998, these long-believed lost scenes were handed over to British producer/director Nick Freand Jones for partial inclusion in his BBC documentary *The Fear Of God: 25 Years Of The Exorcist*. It fell to Freand Jones to piece together and effectively re-edit these sequences, unseen for a quarter of a century.

"Warner Brothers sent us a thick wodge of paper that represented all the footage of the film," Freand Jones says, explaining his own archaeological dig, albeit one of celluloid rather than demonic amulets and St Joseph's medallions. "So we were able to identify sections of film from the vault. What we got was very raw footage, so sometimes there was missing sound, sometimes there were missing shots, so you couldn't even compile the scenes properly. So it took several attempts. But eventually we got to the point where we could reconstruct those scenes quite effectively. The spider walk we had to cheat because there were certain reaction shots missing. The *Casablanca* ending – everything was there apart from sound on the very final exchange. All they had was street sound; they'd never looped that sound.

"The hardest scene we had to construct was the conversation between the doctor and Chris MacNeil early on where she's told that what's wrong with Regan is a 'nervous disorder'. There were masses of takes and we had no template on how to construct it so we just tried to follow the pacing of the film elsewhere and selected what seemed to us the best takes. It's quite a good scene, but again it doesn't really advance things. It makes explicit things I think you pick up anyway. Almost all these scenes, when you look at them individually, they would diminish the atmosphere which I find so admirable in the film. I think the film that's there now is the right film. Yes, the spider walk is interesting and if they could've found a way of working it in at the right place it would've added. And if I could restore any of them, that's the scene I would put back in. And maybe the theological exchange on the stairs. Even to this day, Blatty would like that scene back in the movie. And in a sense that would be the easiest to restore because it would work dramatically and it would sit in where it's supposed to, and it's short. It's the most practical scene to restore. But it's rare that tinkering round like this after the event really improves things. I think the film really stands up as it is."

"I have seen these scenes that have been unearthed," Friedkin adds. "I have no particular objection to them. I still think that the cut of the film as it is now is the best cut of the film, but some of those scenes are kinda nice and I don't know whether it's nostalgia or what, but if I had to, I would put them back in today. I don't think it would hurt anything. But again, I believe that *The Exorcist* is a kind of masterpiece and it's defined in a way as much by what's left out as what is included."

As a coda, there is still a vast amount of footage from *The Exorcist* that remains unseen, as Dick Smith explained: "Owen Roizman had his cameraman shoot a lot of great stuff – background stuff, putting on Linda's make-up and things like that. But he didn't tell Billy. Billy was very much against having any photographs taken. He wouldn't let anyone take any pictures of Linda on the set. He was very secretive. Anyway, when the whole thing was over, Owen screened some of this stuff to me and it was wonderful stuff, but he made a big psychological mistake. He fully intended to get permission before doing anything with it, but he was excited about making a documentary on the making of the film and he told his agent. Unfortunately his agent is also Billy's agent. So immediately Billy is informed and Billy hits the ceiling and comes down on Owen like a ton of bricks because he felt Owen was pulling a fast one on him. And Billy never forgave him for that."

Max von Sydow appearing larger than life

CHAPTER FIFTEEN

LOLAPAZUZU

The American ratings board, the Motion Picture Association Of America (MPAA), screened a rough, unmixed cut of *The Exorcist* on 3 October 1973 and passed it with an 'R' rating meaning 'Restricted', i.e. no one under seventeen was to be admitted without a parent or adult present.

"There was no problem with getting an 'R' rating at all," Friedkin explains. "The ratings board was then being run by a very sensitive, intelligent guy named Aaron Stern. He had a very strong control over his board. Stern went to see *The Exorcist* with his board and he called me a half hour after they finished screening it and he said 'Congratulations. I think it's a great film. We're going to give you an 'R' rating with no cuts. We're not asking for one frame to be cut.' Warners and I thought the whole film would be cut to ribbons to get an 'R', which we had to do. We could not release it as an 'X' picture – they wouldn't do it. So I anticipated a lot of editing as a result of the ratings screening. But he said 'We're gonna give you an 'R', no cuts. I think we're gonna get a lot of heat for this and I think you will as well. But this film should be seen as you made it. It's deserving and good luck to you.' No subsequent ratings board would have given it an 'R' without cuts."

Still the spectre of the new obscenity legislation hung over the movie and Blatty found himself constantly defending the movie

The original film poster

WILLIAM PETER BLATTY'S

THE EXORCIST

Directed by WILLIAM FRIEDKIN

Something almost beyond comprehension is happening to a girl on this street, in this house
...and a man has been sent for as a last resort. This man is The Exorcist.

ELLEN BURSTYN · MAX VON SYDOW · LEE J. COBB
KITTY WINN · JACK MacGOWRAN   JASON MILLER as Father Karras
LINDA BLAIR as Regan · Produced by WILLIAM PETER BLATTY
Executive Producer NOEL MARSHALL · Screenplay by WILLIAM PETER BLATTY based on his novel
From Warner Bros. A Warner Communications Company **R** RESTRICTED Under 17 requires accompanying Parent or Adult Guardian

before its release, while he was promoting his new book *I'll Tell Them I Remember You*, a reminiscence of his late mother. "Let me tell you how *The Exorcist* novel was received," he told one interviewer. "The former Chancellor of the Catholic Church for the City of New York, who is now pastor at Sacred Heart, made *The Exorcist* required reading for his parish. In fact, the novel was taught by nuns in some Catholic high school. Nuns! Any community that decides that it wants to ban *The Exorcist* deserves the punishment of never seeing the film, unless they leave their grubby little towns. You'll find the novelty of the act vanishes, and then the little minds will no longer be interested. Furthermore, this picture could never be construed as appealing to prurient interests."

Something else started happening in the run-up to the release of *The Exorcist*. More and more stories began to appear in the press, not just more inflated, fanciful pieces about the so-called 'curse' behind the movie, but stories about the making of the film, its budget overruns, the alleged infighting. Lalo Schifrin talked to *The Hollywood Reporter* about his dismissal from the film: "My score, I stand by it, is one of the best I've ever done. I had not the opportunity to record it. He [Friedkin] only listened to three or four cues, and he walked off. Everybody there loved it. I was applauded by the musicians, which happens very seldom in Hollywood."

The rift between Blatty and Friedkin, and the former's supposed barring from the editing process, also became the stuff of tabloid fare, with talk of Blatty taking legal recourse. Executive producer Noel Marshall told *The Hollywood Reporter* that Blatty was indeed taking legal action over "the firing of Schifrin and other differences, presumably including his alleged barring by Friedkin from post-production editing and dubbing." Even the possessory credit on the film – Blatty wanted it billed as 'William Peter Blatty's *The Exorcist*' although normally the director takes such a credit – was making the news. Before anyone had seen it, *The Exorcist* was becoming an event. The movie itself was now the story, not the story of the movie. It didn't matter what was true, just as it didn't matter later who did or didn't faint, throw up, etc. whilst watching the film. *The Exorcist* was moving movies beyond simple entertainment. Now they were news and cinema would never be the same again.

The film was previewed, a few days before its release, at a screening held at the Directors' Guild of America. Present were a mix of public, Warner Brothers' executives and the movie's publicist Joe Hyams. (As the screening began, the final reel wasn't there as Billy was still mixing it down the street. It arrived just in time.) "Shortly after the film started somebody screamed some obscenities from the first row and at that point I remember getting out of my seat and moving to the back of the theatre," Hyams told the BBC. "Now at a certain moment in the film – it's when the girl's having her examination – the first person comes past me heading for the rest room. And he gets sick in the rest room. I asked him if he was feeling better and he said 'Yes, I am. I should not have had Mexican food.' A couple of minutes later another person comes running out and I ask them if they had Mexican food. Now after a while, five or six people physically get sick. Other people could not watch it and were just white and faint. I just thought: how do we keep this story from spreading? The last thing we want is a film that is making people sick. And my management was all in one row and I remember their heads were turning, watching what was happening. The film ends and seven or eight of our top executives are seated alone in the theatre. One gentleman, a high-level executive, suggested that it might be best if we shelve the film and never distribute it. He thought it was just totally obscene and should not be shown to people. They talked about it for about five minutes and shot down the idea. Then they said 'What happened here tonight Joe?' I said 'I don't know.' They said 'Why were people running up and down the aisles?' I said 'They were getting sick.' They said 'We have to put a lid on this, people getting sick at this film.' Then I said 'Fellas, I don't know what happened tonight. I saw the same film. All I can tell you is the other 900 people who saw this film are all congregated outside this theatre talking about it. Not one person has gotten in their car to leave yet. You can't get into any of the bars across the street because they're packed with people. That's what you got fellas, *that's* your movie.' "

When the film was released, the day after Christmas 1973, it didn't disappoint. The end justified the hype and propelled it to unheard-of levels. "We literally finished *The Exorcist* three days before it opened," Friedkin said at the time. "Frankly, if there hadn't been an opening date I'd still be working on it. Given the chance, I'd have had all the actors in the booth on opening night with microphones, changing and fine-tuning it. Actually, I'd still be working on *The French Connection* if somebody hadn't said 'Get it out of here and into the theatres.' I just always want to make it that much better."

Despite mixed reviews, and Friedkin's perfectionism, the movie that opened was greeted with unprecedented audience reaction. People came, they saw, they threw up, they fainted, in one case they miscarried a baby, in others they sought psychiatric aid or spiritual counselling. Then they queued up outside the theatre for up to four hours to do it all again. Playing in just two theatres – one in New York, one in LA – the film took a record $94,003.50 from 28,183 admissions in its first week.

"I was present the first time somebody fainted," recalls Blatty. "It was at the first preview in New York. I was nervously standing at the back and this woman came up the aisle, with her hand over her face and she kept murmuring 'Jesus, Jesus.' And I remember thinking 'I hope that's not Pauline Kael.' I thought we were in deep trouble. But the point that she walked out on was the scene at which I never look – the artereogram scene. I only watched it once when I had to see it on the movieola in the rough cut. I've never looked at it since. And actually, that's the scene that caused most of the getting weak and fainting. When the head spins and whatever, they're having a wonderful rollercoaster ride."

Cinema managers were forced to lay on smelling salts. Frank Kveton, a cinema manager in Oakbrook claimed "My janitors are going crazy wiping up the vomit." A minister in the same town proudly noted "We turned them away in hundreds from my *Exorcist* sermon" as church attendance rose dramatically. Heart attacks whilst watching the film were reported. In Berkeley a man was injured as he charged the screen attempting to "get" the demon; in Boston several young men paraded naked before the screen insisting they *were* the Devil. In New York they lit fires on the street to keep warm whilst waiting several hours to get in. Ticket touts were charging up to $50 for a pair of tickets; one cinema security guard claimed he was offered bribes of up to $110 to let people in. Box office records fell, and continued to fall, as more and more theatres were added to meet the demand. In Washington the 'R' rating was overturned and no one under seventeen was allowed in; in Boston the film was given the dreaded 'X' rating. And in Chicago, six people were reported to have ended up in a psychiatric ward after seeing the film. Still the people came. Donald Rugoff, president of the Cinema 5 chain, said "I don't think there's been anything like it in the history of the business." The *Toronto Medical Post* reported that, after viewing the movie, four women were confined to psychiatric care. A Chicago psychiatrist publicly declared "There is no way you can sit through that film without receiving some lasting negative or disturbing effects." The film crossed all social boundaries, attracting a large black audience in the inner cities, something that Warners hadn't anticipated. (Jason Miller later told Mark Kermode about visiting a black friend of his in Harlem who dragged him along to a cinema showing the movie: "I said 'Are you kidding me? I don't wanna go and see *The Exorcist*.' He said 'No, you gotta see this. I don't want you to see the film. I want you to see the audience.' So we go in and there's like maybe 200 blacks in the audience – and they've got lunches. And they've got beer and they're passing joints, and *The Exorcist* is on. It was like this colony of people, they went and they spent all afternoon watching this film, bringing lunch in, bringing pizza in, talking, yelling, reading lines. And that probably to me was the epitome of the power of the film. That for these people they had to be around it. It was like being around the totem pole, something sacred to them.")

"I would say the first five, six, seven, eight weeks of the showing of the film the same reaction occurred as happened that night we showed the film at the Directors' Guild," says Joe Hyams. "Some people leaving the theatre, becoming sick and so on. Then after seven or eight weeks, it kind of settled down. People were braver and whatever created that phenomenon kinda went away at that time. Did I play it up? Sure, I played it up in the sense that people wanted to know how many people got sick last night. I would inflate the figures. That was my job. There was nothing I could do to kill that picture, so I'd lie a little. But that was the extent of it. There was really nothing we had to do that wasn't happening by itself. Which is what happens on an event movie. It just transcends everything and anything publicists and marketing people can do."

Six months after its release, Warners expanded its run to 110 theatres in the New York area, bringing in a first week sum of over $3 million, and forever changing the nature of film distribution in America, by taking quality movies and opening them on more and more screens, something that was to prove a hugely important factor in the release of such subsequent event movies as *Jaws* and *Star Wars*, and the blockbuster era that *The Exorcist* gave birth to. Still the hysteria continued. Evangelist Billy Graham went as far as to say that there was evil present in the actual celluloid of the movie.

Blatty, for one, was stunned by the whole reaction: "Completely. And to this day I do not understand it. I look at Billy Graham's comments that there was a power of evil in the film and I thought that he was mad. But you know, he was on to something. I think what he was trying to express is that there is an explosive power in the film and the fact is that it is greater than the sum of its parts. It's that X factor. I don't know what that is. People say things like 'Ah, there are subliminal images, they're brainwashing us. There are things that our consciousness does not see but our unconsciousness is comprehending and that's the secret of the power of the film. It's none of that; there are no subliminal images. If you can see it, it's not subliminal."

In trade bible *Variety*, Rabbi Julius G. Neumann was quoted as saying: "This movie is adding to the frustration and confusion of our youth by claiming that whatever they do, contrary to accepted religious or society's norm, is not really of their own making but that of the Devil inside of them." Blatty responded to the hysteria by saying "There are a lot of neurotic people. I may well be one of them. If they read the book, or see the film, neither experience makes them neurotic. To my mind, they were neurotic to begin with. Now they have a name for their neurosis. They say 'I'm possessed.' Anyone who is mentally unstable should not see the film, whether it's a child or an adult."

Warners proudly predicted that the film would outgross the $34 million haul of *My Fair Lady*, up until then the company's biggest ever money spinner; industry pundits predicted it would outgross the $85 million made the previous year by Francis Ford Coppola's *The Godfather*, making it the biggest movie of all time.

The New York Times got on line for an extensive report from the queue outside one New York theatre where 'people stood like sheep in the rain, in cold and sleet for up to four hours to see the chilling film about a twelve-year-old girl going to the Devil.' *The Times* found a wide cross-section waiting in line – from a sixty-eight-year-old woman ("I have never stood in line for any movie or any restaurant before in my life"), to a forty-six-year-old housewife ("I haven't stood in line since the time I saw Frank Sinatra"), to a large contingent of teens and twentysomethings, including Jack Fletcher, a nineteen-year-old student, who said "You feel contaminated when you leave the theatre. There's something that is impossible to erase. I've had nightmares ever since I've seen it." Another person interviewed on 'the line' was the actor William Hurt, then a twenty-three-year-old Juliard drama student 'who talked more like a sociologist' when quizzed about his reasons for standing on line: "It makes the movie better, right? The more you pay for something, the more it's worth. And it also has to do with telling your friends that you've seen it."

Harvard sociologist Howard Reisman, author of *The Lonely Crowd*, argued that standing in line in such a manner was a good way for strangers to meet in a city: "Standing in a movie line doesn't commit you to having a motive. It's a relationship that doesn't ask too much. In a singles bar there is a motive, and people who go there are subject to interpretations and misinterpretations. For example, a single woman at a singles bar might feel that people will think she's there as date-bait. The 'standing on one foot' conversation that she might have with a stranger in a movie line might be more comfortable for her."

Events on 'the line' weren't always so convivial. One cinema was forced to close its doors when the crowd, fearing that after hours of waiting they would not make it into the last screening of the day, started to riot. This astonishing reaction to *The Exorcist* was repeated worldwide, although news reports took a distinctly darker tone when the film arrived in Europe. John Power, a sixteen-year-old London boy, suffered a fatal epileptic fit the day after seeing the film with his girlfriend, prompting numerous 'Boy Dies After Seeing *The Exorcist*' style tabloid headlines. Seventeen-year-old Nicolas Bell claimed he had become 'possessed' after seeing the film and killed nine-year-old Sandra Simpson. Bell said in his defence: "It was not really me that did it. There was something inside me. I want to see a priest. It is ever since I saw that film, *The Exorcist*. I felt something take possession of me. It has been in me ever since." In West Germany, nineteen-year-old Rainer Hertrampf's suicide was blamed on the movie, leading to calls for it to be banned. Back in England, screenings of the film were picketed by an unspecified evangelical organisation who handed out leaflets proclaiming "We can't stop you seeing this film, but you should know the film bears the power of evil". The front of their four-page booklet featured a quote attributed to the Western Psychiatric Institute of Pittsburgh, USA ("after admitting twelve new patients"), "Some people who never before needed mental treatment were falling apart after seeing this film." Over the page an unnamed twenty-three-year-old Cambridge graduate insisted that "anyone who sees this film runs the risk of serious mental and spiritual danger and disturbance."

Billy Friedkin had set out to make a provocative film, but even for him, things got out of hand: "I remember reading that a classmate of Prince Charles saw the film and immolated himself on the alter of a church in England. Then there were also stories like James Cagney the actor. I met him at an American Film Institute lunch and he told me that he hadn't seen *The Exorcist* but his barber had. This man was his barber for twenty-five years. He saw the film, quit being a barber and went off to enter the priesthood. There were a lot of stories like that. The reactions were much more extreme than I thought. I thought the reactions both pro and con did get a bit extreme."

Blatty found himself on the receiving end of the hysterical reaction to the film on several occasions: "I used to appear quite frequently on the *Tonight Show*," he explains "And there were stories of pictures falling off walls when I would appear, or marble tables cracking in two, and on and on and on. And I would yawn . . . but there were two appearances on the *Tonight Show* back to back in which the first time they lost the picture, and Johnny Carson leaned over and told me that this had never happened before. Of course we were talking about *The Exorcist* at the time, and the next time, they lost the sound. And then somewhere in that period, I was invited to dinner by Richard Pryor, and there were a lovely group of people there and after dinner my wife and I were sitting on the sofa facing the fireplace. And above the mantle was an enormous oil painting that hung from a very thick ingot that must have been about four to five inches long and affixed by a strong leather band. Now Richard Pryor is offering me coffee, standing there with a tray with cream and sugar on it, and suddenly there's this massive crash behind him. He looked and the painting had come off. There is now dead silence in the room, nobody speaks and everybody's trying not to look at me, until Richard says 'Sugar?' We then examine this thing – the ingot is in place; the leather band that held the painting in place was unbroken. It was very bizarre."

Needless to say, now that it was out there, the film bred more controversy. The United States Catholic Conference publicly criticised the MPAA for allowing the film its 'R' rating. In Boston, Mrs Rita Warren took the film to court in an attempt to get it banned, citing it as obscene and blasphemous: "We are the community. The community has been offended by this film and it must be stopped." The action was eventually dismissed.

In Washington, where the movie had filmed, a seventeen years and older restriction was accompanied by police action, with threats to arrest anyone who attempted to take a minor into the cinema, or sell a ticket to a minor.

The New York Times ran an article also criticising the MPAA's rating, forcing MPAA President Jack Valenti to issue a rebuttal: "Ratings come from what viewers see, not what they imagine they see. In *The Exorcist*, there is no overt sex; there is no excessive violence. There is some strong language, but it is rationally related to the film's themes and is kept to a minimum. *The Exorcist* deals in the metaphysical unknown, always terrifying because it cannot be defined or readily comprehended."

It was through another piece in *The New York Times* that Mercedes McCambridge threw her oar in. Dissatisfied with what she saw as a betrayal by Friedkin over her lack of credit on the movie, McCambridge went public, outing herself as the voice of the Devil and criticising Linda Blair into the bargain. "Her vocal performance was laughable," the actress said. "I gave the most difficult performance of my life and then Warners didn't give me a single credit on the picture or in the advertising. The man who supplied the *jewels* got a credit. I *cried*. Billy Friedkin promised me a special credit – 'And Mercedes McCambridge.' He broke his promise – it's heartbreaking when someone you thought was a *friend* does that. I put my father's crucifix against my forehead just twenty minutes ago. It was ice-cold, and I thought 'God has deserted me. Shall I go off on an ocean cruise?'

"I'm a product of sixteen years of convent education and I am still a devout Catholic, so speaking those vile blaspheming words was an *agony* for me. . . . So you see, after all I went through why I'm mad at Billy Friedkin for not getting me on those credits. Any child could have wiggled on the bed. *If there was any horror in the exorcism, it was me!*"

Billy Friedkin replied angrily to the story: "In our conversation I said 'Now if you really do this thing right, no one will realise that the voice was dubbed,' and she agreed. Her contract called for no credit and she admitted that it wasn't important. When the picture came out and was this enormous success, she evidently changed her mind and did that hysterical interview with someone at *The New York Times*. She seemed to be saying that she thought God was punishing her for doing the demon's voice, but it could be all put right if she got a credit.

"I agree she was entitled to credit," he continued, "But where she is off the mark and wrong, and where she has committed the most unprofessional action I've ever seen, is where she tries to diminish Linda Blair's contribution. Linda Blair worked on that film for over a year. She did every scene in that film herself, created the role, worked at it. I mean every actor and every technician that was there can verify that.

"All of a sudden it was everything about Mercedes McCambridge," Blair told the BBC. "She did the voice so they tried to pull my nomination for an Academy Award. It was an awful time after the film was released because everything was 'Did Linda Blair really do the film?' So I'd gone through everything I'd gone through, and it's quite obvious beneath the make-up it's me, and the voice is a mixture of Mercedes and I. And my hat's off to Mercedes for the work that she did. I know what she went through and doggone it, yes, she should be recognised for that. But I was very much a part of that."

Blair's contribution to the movie was called into further doubt when her double – Eileen Dietz – decided to speak up next, this time in an open letter to *Variety*, petitioning the Screen Actor's Guild 'simply for the right to talk about the work I filmed.' Friedkin, eager to stand up for his young star, attacked Ms Dietz's claims on the *Barry Gray* radio show: "Linda Blair's stand-in – Eileen Dietz – decided to build a career on the false claim that she played some of the demonic scenes in the picture. She was a stand-in and a photo double in a handful of scenes that last a few seconds on the screen. Her contributions – ten shots – totalled twenty-eight seconds in a film that lasts two hours. It's like when you see a film in which the guys are playing poker and there's a close-up of the hands. You use a double for the hands. It's a common practice."

Blair spoke up for herself soon enough, instructing her lawyers to petition the Screen Actor's Guild to arbitrate the matter, forcing Dietz to back away. "Nobody could have anticipated the kind of horrendous attention that Linda got after making the film," says Ellen Burstyn, "And how difficult it was for her to handle. I think we were all protective during the making of the film – we all saw that as a difficult thing for her – but that turned out to be the easy part. The hard part was, I think, the fame that came from it."

Just to add to the litigious fervour, Warner Brothers also got involved, taking action against *Newsweek* magazine which broke Friedkin's embargo on printing pictures of Blair in demon make-up, which they had obtained by snapping them directly off the screen in a local theatre.

Inevitably, as the various controversies surrounding the movie grew, so did the stories about it's so-called curse.

William Friedkin

THE 'CURSE' OF THE EXORCIST

Stories citing *The Exorcist* as a 'cursed' film began while the movie was still in production, and persist to this day, lending the film a mystique that remains unique.

Blatty joked that the whole thing started with an interview Friedkin gave to *Newsweek*, with the director indulging a distinct case of 'ass-covering', given how over-budget and over-schedule his film had become: "No, that's total bullshit" is Friedkin's succinct reply to that theory.

The Exorcist was a movie steeped in its own mythology from day one. As the film grew, so did the myth. From heart attacks in the cinema to heart attacks on set, the story was a good one, moreover an appropriate one. At the time, everyone involved was eager to spur it on. Friedkin may now dismiss it out of hand – and quite rightly so – but looking back at the interviews he gave around the time, they confirm him as a master showman. He often talked about having seen a magician cut his assistant in half prior to filming. This wasn't a casual supper club magic act; this cutting in half involved blood, guts, the whole shebang. The audience's collective jaw dropped as the assistant appeared to lie in her own viscera and the magician took his bows. Only afterwards, the magician had to explain that what they had seen was an illusion, no matter how good it was. Friedkin learned from that man. His talk of magnetic fields 'levitating'

Ellen Burstyn

Linda Blair is only part of it. He didn't fan the flames, but he certainly didn't try to put the fire out.

Chief culprit in propagating the curse of *The Exorcist* was unit publicist Howard Newman, whose long out-of-print book, *The Exorcist: The Strange Story Behind The Film*, single-handedly makes a veritable art form out of coincidence. Stories abound on the level of one crew member's pet hamster having died forty-five years before the filming of *The Exorcist* – in mysterious circumstances. Fair enough, that was Newman's job. Friedkin after all had banned all press from the set and wasn't allowing anyone to see pictures of Blair in make-up. Newman needed to talk the movie up; he succeeded.

The 'curse' of *The Exorcist* boils down to a number of incidents which occurred in a group of people's lives over roughly a twelve- to eighteen-month period, and these include: Jason Miller's son was hit by a motorbike on the beach, Max von Sydow's brother died, Linda Blair's grandfather died, a gaffer lost a toe, the set burned down twice, the first set was not up to scratch design-wise (hardly the work of the Devil, but included nonetheless), Ellen Burstyn damaged her back, Bill Blatty's secretary Noni was mysteriously taken ill, whilst her roommate was apparently carted off in a straitjacket, having gone insane. As the film's impact was felt, this mythology grew. There was talk of hidden images in the subliminal edits, talk of double exposures appearing in the rushes, Friedkin's initial desire to 'hide' the voice of the demon and, of course, the various vomitings, faintings, miscarriages and the all-in, all-out audience reactions, all unprecedented, that greeted the film's arrival in theatres.

Ellen Burstyn, for one, finds something in the 'curse' that the film attracted: "During the course of the film there were nine deaths," she told the BBC in 1998, "Which is an enormous amount of deaths connected with the film. Some very directly, like Jack MacGowran, who gets killed in the film. He completed shooting and died. And in the film it's the assistant director who comes to Chris MacNeil's house and tells her that that character has been killed, and in life it was the assistant director who called me and told me about Jack's death, and all I could think of was that it was strange enough that Jack had died, but it was even more strange that I was hearing it from the assistant director as I did in the film.

"I think Linda Blair's grandfather died in the course of the shooting," the actress continues, warming to the topic. "Max von Sydow's brother died. The assistant cameraman whose wife had a baby during the shoot, the baby died. The man who refrigerated the set died; the young black nightwatchman was accidentally shot by a policeman, who thought he was pulling a gun. Jason Miller's son, who had a brain operation the year before, was on the beach, buried up to his neck in the sand, when a motorcycle ran over his head. I don't remember all of the others, but there were nine and that's too many. The set caught on fire one weekend when no one was there. I had brought some chants and music and prayers on tape from a spiritual group I belonged to, which I planned to use if things got too weird. They were stolen out of my dressing room – the tape recorder and the tapes were stolen."

Burstyn of course also suffered serious back damage during filming: "In the scene where Linda slaps me across the face and I go flying across the room and land on the floor, I had a rig around my midriff with a wire coming out the back, and the stuntman was pulling me into the floor. And we did one take and afterwards I said 'Billy, he's pulling me too hard. I can get hurt.' And Billy said 'Well, it has to look real.' And I said 'I know it has to look real, but I'm telling you I could get hurt. He's pulling me too hard.' And the stuntman was standing there, listening to this and Billy said to him 'OK, don't pull her so hard.' But as I turned away, I felt them exchange a look where Billy was saying 'Pull her!' And he pulled me into the floor and I landed on my spine and it was damaged permanently. I still have trouble with it. I screamed in horrendous pain and Billy motioned to Owen to tilt the camera down on me, to photograph my screams. I saw it and I was so furious that he did that. Even though I couldn't talk because I was screaming so hard, I still used an obscene word and said 'Turn that fucking camera off' because I couldn't stand that he was willing to get a quick shot of it before he called the ambulance. I was on crutches for the next three weeks. I don't think I missed any shooting, but I was on crutches and I would get off them to go do the scene, and then come back at the edge of the shooting area and be back on crutches. It was very painful."

Despite the trauma involving his son, Jason Miller is less quick to buy into the notion of the film as damaged goods. As he explained during the making of the documentary *The Fear Of God*, a certain incident that happened early in the shoot sticks with him. "When I was filming I would go to this little restaurant in the Jesuit quarter of Georgetown and sit there and study my lines. One day this very, very old priest came in. I think his name was Father MacGowran. He'd seen my play *That Championship Season* on Broadway and he was very complimentary, and he handed me this little medal of the blessed virgin and he said 'Wear this during the filming.' And I said 'OK, thanks Father, I will.' And he said 'Do you know why I'm giving you this? I'm going to tell you something about intervention. Did you ever hear of the concept of intervention? It's a nasty concept that comes out of the 15th century – if you do anything on the Devil to reveal him as the trickster that he is, he will seek retribution against you. He will even try to stop what you're trying to do to unmask him.' And he said 'This medal will protect you.'

"Maybe about three days later, I'm walking past these Jesuit halls and I see a casket in there. And I walk back and I look in the room and there is an old priest in the casket – dead. And it's the priest who gave me the medal. And then my son got injured on the beach. I think he was dead for a couple of seconds, because all his body functions went and everything like that. And it popped into my mind while I'm trying to give him mouth-to-mouth, what that old priest said."

Joe Hyams, Father Thomas Bermingham and Billy Friedkin witnessed another event while promoting the movie in Italy that pointed (conveniently?) towards the involvement of forces beyond our understanding: "We were playing the film at the Metropolitan Theatre in Rome," Hyams told the BBC. "And at the entrance to the piazza are twin 16th-century churches, with identical crucifixes on top of the churches. I'm at the theatre watching the crowd going in and loving it. And then I heard a noise coming from the piazza, and I walked down and lightning had struck and hit one of the crosses on top of one of the churches. That cross was probably 400 years old. It was very heavy and large, but it fell. I'm a sceptic, but this is really pushing me too much."

For a movie conceived – both in novel form and on screen – in abject realism, there's no denying that hyperbole played a part in the unprecedented success of *The Exorcist*. As to the veracity of this long-believed 'curse', Billy Friedkin probably has the best perspective: "I saw Ellen Burstyn talking about nine people associated with the movie who have died. The assistant cameraman's third cousin – that's a load of shit. People are dying while we're talking. One minute from now you or I could die. It's all written in a book, I believe. Everything is fate – our lives, how we got here – we don't know, when we're gonna leave here – we don't know; it's all taken care of for us and while we're here all we can do is the best we can, to make life better and easier for others that follow us. That seems to me to be the only purpose of being here. But the deaths connected with *The Exorcist* as part of a curse is a load of shit! It's strictly concocted by the media. And most of the people who write stories about movies are so fucking stupid that they have nothing better to write about. They don't know what to say. They can't really deal with any of the profound religious issues, so they write about nine people who died, you know. The second movie I did, *The Night They Raided Minsky's*, the actor Bert Lahr, who was one of the three leads, he died before he finished his role. We had to shoot over the shoulder with a double to complete certain scenes we had shot with him. But we had to write him out of the script, which harmed the film because he had a very important role which had to be shot. Nothing like that happened in *The Exorcist*, where someone died before they'd completed their part or anything. I see Ellen Burstyn saying Jack MacGowran died right after he finished the film. Well, Jack MacGowran had a weak heart. I believe he had a drinking problem. He was not a young man at the time.

"There were certain strange things that happened like the

burning of the set. No one knows how that happened, and the insurance company wasn't able to find out, but they paid off. But not the deaths or anything. And I never offered any of that as an excuse. I mean the film was delayed for six weeks before it could begin filming because the set burned down. And the only theory was that there were pigeons flying around in the rafters and perhaps a pigeon drove into a light box and perhaps caused an electricity short. That was the theory on which the insurance company paid off. But as to the curse, that was total bullshit."

If *The Exorcist* wasn't cursed during filming, it was to a degree afterwards, most notably when it came to that year's Academy Awards. Hundreds of thousands were still queuing round the block when the film's ten nominations were announced. Billy Friedkin, who legend had it had a silhouette of his previous Oscar, with an outline of another accompanied by a question mark, stencilled on his director's chair during the shoot, must have felt confident. All the major participants in the movie were nominated. Linda Blair had already won the Peoples' Choice award and the Golden Globe.

On the night the film walked away with two statuettes out of a possible ten, with the anaemic Paul Newman-Robert Redford period caper comedy *The Sting* taking, amongst others, Best Film and Best Director (for George Roy Hill), actions that for anyone with even a passing interest in film defy anything involving the word 'criteria'.

Billy Friedkin personally feels that the attention-seeking actions of both Mercedes McCambridge and Eileen Dietz cost Linda Blair her Oscar, while those associated with the film feel there was an unofficial campaign against it within the voting Hollywood community.

"I won the Peoples' Choice; I won the Golden Globe. Nobody can take that away from me," Linda Blair told journalist Mark Kermode in 1998. "I was nominated for an Academy Award. But then, all of a sudden, Hollywood's like, wait a minute, we don't want this movie here. And this is what I have read and researched over the years because I really, as an adult, wanted to know what happened. I'm the victim of it, I wanna know what happened. Some very prominent directors, with a lot of power, felt that this was a trash film. It shouldn't be here, and if she didn't do the voice, then take away her nomination. I didn't know any of this – I was protected, thank God. But I'm glad as an adult I know the truth behind it because I didn't know why we weren't winning Academy Awards when it was such a brilliant film."

Twenty-five years on, Billy Friedkin is less concerned with the events of 2 April 1974: "Those are all subjective anyway," says the filmmaker, who already has an Oscar for a bookend. "What is the best of anything? When you get nominated for ten Academy Awards, that's not a rebuff. I look at the ten nominations, not the fact that we lost eight of them in the final awards. I was disappointed certainly, but since there are no ultimate standards as to what is the best of anything in terms of film, I can't complain. The year *French Connection* won I didn't necessarily think it was the best film of the year. But then again, that's subjective. You're fortunate to be singled out in that way and you don't look a gift horse in the mouth. *Citizen Kane* didn't win Best Picture, or Best Director or Best Actor. It's arguably the best of all three of all time when it comes to American film; it's certainly the most influential film of all time when it comes to American film. So rebuff, schmuff, I couldn't care less. I was exhilarated that we got ten nominations on a film that was called a horror film. *Frankenstein* didn't get ten nominations, or *Psycho*."

Bill Blatty did go home with an Oscar that night for Best Adapted Screenplay, yet he remains less forgiving than his director: "I was quite crushed, frustrated by it," the author freely admits. "The bloom was off the rose when it didn't win Best Picture. And I was a young man and I was foolishly intemperate in my comments about all that right afterwards, which I regret. But I really felt that we were robbed. I mean look at the directorial work. And in terms of the challenge, the difficulty of the material – therefore the achievement. How can you compare the winning film that year with what Bill Friedkin did? It was a job every heavyweight director in the country was afraid to tackle, too tough for them. I felt awful."

By then, of course it didn't matter. *The Exorcist*, an adult-themed, deeply disturbing meditation on the mysteries of faith had surpassed *Gone With The Wind*, *The Sound Of Music* and *The Godfather* as the biggest box office draw of all time.

In 1998 I asked Billy Friedkin if he felt the film represented his best work. Much to my surprise, he answered such a limiting question: "In terms of its impact, yes. In terms of its cast, absolutely. In terms of what it has to say and the message it continues to deliver to audiences around the world, yes. And those are very important standards. It's probably the one film of mine that I directed that I can still look at without cringing. And it's because of its story. The story is great, the characters are terrific, we had a great cast to bring it off. What did I try to do for the most part? Stay out of their way. I have what is known as – and I've had it for some time – the surgeon's credo 'First, do no harm'. It was my credo on that film – 'Don't fuck this up'. In terms of technique in the film, the technique is almost invisible and that I'm proud of. Ernest Hemingway once said he had no real technique. What critics think of as his technique is really little more than to cover a certain lack of talent in certain areas. And that'd how I viewed *The Exorcist*."

EXORCIST II: THE HERETIC

I t's almost impossible to imagine from a modern perspective that there was once a time when Hollywood was naive about sequels. If today's maxim is: bigger, better, faster, more, then back in those days it was: cheaper, tackier and considerably less. Sequelising a success was not considered the norm and when it was done – as with the *Planet Of The Apes* series, for example – it was generally considered to be a case of diminishing returns for less and less investment. Only with Francis Ford Coppola's *The Godfather Part II* in 1974 and John Frankenheimer's follow-up to Friedkin's *The French Connection* in the following year, would Hollywood begin to see that a sequel could enhance or even eclipse its original, both artistically and commercially. It was somewhere between these two stools that Warner Brothers decided that a sequel to *The Exorcist* should be made.

"Warners did approach me and at that time I thought: the story is over," says Bill Blatty. "Karras fell down the steps; he's dead – the story is over. There is no sequel possible. So I declined."

Friedkin too had no desire to return to the tale, but Linda Blair, now pushing adulthood, tentatively agreed to a follow-up, depending on the script, and so wheels were set in motion.

"What we essentially wanted to do with the sequel was to redo the first movie," the film's co-producer Richard Lederer said at the

Linda Blair practices her possession scene with co-star Richard Burton

time. "Have the central figure, an investigative priest, interview everyone involved in the exorcism, then fade out to unused footage, unused angles from the first movie. A low-budget rehash – about $3 million – of *The Exorcist*, a rather cynical approach to movie-making, I'll admit. But that was the start."

In Blatty's absence, playwright William Goodheart was commissioned to write a screenplay titled *The Heretic*. Goodheart hit upon the teachings of Teilhard de Chardin, the French archaeologist who had provided, in part, the inspiration for the character of Merrin, as his starting point. As Goodheart began to base his screenplay around de Chardin's concept of the world-mind – the notion that one day all our minds will evolve to form a telepathic whole – the scale of the project broadened.

Warners were eager to sign a name director and following such acclaimed movies as *Point Blank* and *Deliverance,* British filmmaker John Boorman soon topped that list. "I had a Jesuit education and the idea of making a metaphysical thriller greatly appealed to my psyche," Boorman said. The director made it a condition of his contract that he could make the film wherever he wanted to. At that time Boorman planned to film all the interiors at the National Film Studios of Ireland, where he was based. Years before, Warners executive John Calley had shown him a copy of Blatty's original novel when the studio was still casting around for a director. "I turned it down because as a film I thought it would be rather repulsive," Boorman explained in a TV interview at the time. "I told Calley 'Not only will I not make this movie but I don't want you to make it either.'

"The idea of making a film that drew on the expectations of an existing audience is what I found exciting," he continued, explaining his reasons for agreeing to make a sequel to another director's acclaimed work. "Every film has to struggle to find a connection with its audience. Here I saw the chance to make an extremely ambitious film without having to spend the time developing this connection. I could make assumptions and then take the audience on a very adventurous cinematic journey."

Boorman attempted to rewrite the script with Goodheart but it soon became clear that things weren't working out. A research trip to the Vatican had shown the filmmaker that they would not be able to film there; similarly, civil unrest in Ethiopia, where a large part of the movie was to take place, meant that filming there would also not be possible. Warner Brothers increasingly wanted the film to be shot on their Burbank backlot and now, with many of the movie's key exteriors having to be set-bound, this became the case. Unhappy with the way Goodheart's script was going, Boorman brought in Rospo Pallenberg, a former collaborator from *Deliverance*. (Pallenberg would later receive the somewhat unique credit 'Creative Associate' for his contribution to the script.) "He developed a structure of which I approved," Boorman explained to Pallenberg's wife Barbara, who chronicled the making of the movie "And we got a new version of the script that was done much too fast. . . . We gave it to Goodheart, who didn't like it at all, of course. I wanted Goodheart to do a rewrite based on this new structure but it soon became clear that this wouldn't work. It was too different, he thought, from his own sensibilities. We began to spend hours arguing over a single line of dialogue."

Goodheart and Boorman soon ceased collaborating and the director reworked the script with Pallenberg. (Bill Blatty was shown a copy of Goodheart's original screenplay by Warners: "They ran a story by me that involved going back in time to Merrin's first exorcism and I said 'OK.' After that nobody showed me anything.")

The unexpected death of Lee J. Cobb led to further rewriting of the script as Lieutenant Kinderman was to have been a major character in the sequel. When Ellen Burstyn confirmed that she would not be repeating her Oscar-nominated role as Chris MacNeil, Kitty Winn's character – Sharon – was resurrected and added to the mix, largely at Warner's insistence. The studio's concern was that their sequel was showing fewer and fewer ties to the original film. Max von Sydow initially turned the project down flat as he was concerned over the negative impact that the original movie had had. However, Boorman eventually persuaded him to change his mind.

By now it was early 1976, the film was due to start shooting in

April, and still the production team had no workable script. Alongside Regan, the central character of *The Heretic* was to be Father Lamont, a priest investigating the circumstances surrounding the death of Father Merrin some years before. Boorman's *Deliverance* star, Jon Voight was originally in line to play the role. Voight made several suggestions as to how to develop the screenplay, but eventually backed out of the project. David Carradine, Jack Nicholson and a young, then unknown, Christopher Walken were all considered for the role. Richard Burton meanwhile was in the midst of a huge Broadway success in Peter Shaffer's play *Equus*. The role was offered to him and he accepted, which required another rewrite from Pallenberg as Lamont had previously been seen as a young man. The role of Dr Gene Tuskin, Regan's psychologist, also underwent a major change. It had been conceived as a male part, with Chris Sarandon, George Segal and, once again, David Carradine, all in the running for the role. Eventually it was decided to turn Dr Tuskin into a woman and Louise Fletcher, who had just won an Oscar for her role in *One Flew Over The Cuckoo's Nest*, was cast.

Budgeted at $12.5 million, *Exorcist II: The Heretic* began filming on 24 May 1976. Boorman had by now decided to film the vast majority of his movie not on location, as he had originally planned, but on sound stages. He intended to give the film a unique visual style that would, at least, set it apart from the documentarian eye of Friedkin's first instalment.

"When you work on location," the director explained "You tend to seek out strange configurations in the landscape, anything out of the ordinary, and you shoot it with the assurance that it is real. You concentrate on using the qualities that appeal to you. The tendency on a set however, is to make everything look ordinary because you start to worry that otherwise it won't look 'real'. My word to Richard [MacDonald, production designer] on this set was: Make it look as daring as possible, and the reality would take care of itself."

The elaborate sets would eventually include such diverse locations as the labyrinthine, all-glass maze of Dr Tuskin's office, a vertical rock chimney which both von Sydow and Burton would be required to climb, an Ethiopian village beset by a swarm of locusts and a church carved into the rock on a mountain top.

However, the eventual script of *The Heretic* was a confused tale that found Father Lamont (sent by the Vatican to examine the nature of Merrin's death) drawn to Regan. She is now involved in a series of experiments with a hypnotic device called a Synchroniser that allows the priest to link with her dreams and memories, re-experiencing the events of the first movie and also, of Merrin's first encounter with Pazuzo in Africa many years before. (Ironically, this time around, von Sydow required no old age make-up for the majority of his appearance.) The movie was due to shoot for fifteen weeks.

During the shoot, Linda Blair was eternally optimistic, if a little less naive than the first time around: "I didn't want to do the demon make-up again, for two reasons. First, I was afraid that my face would die – I'm very lucky that it didn't die the first time. And I knew I didn't have to do it again; my position had changed.

"I think both John Boorman and Billy Friedkin are geniuses," she explained to Barbara Pallenberg. "John, I think, will be more visual and not into the performance, and I do like help with the performance. Billy was my first teacher and I would really like to work with him again." (For brief shots of Regan in Demon make-up, a double was used.)

Midway through production, Boorman contracted a dose of San Joaquin Valley Fever, derived from the dust used on the African sets, that put him – and the production – out of action for over a month. This was at considerable cost to the studio and there was the constant threat that the production might have to be closed down. Burton was due to move straight into the movie of *Equus* and it was uncertain whether the production, now seriously overrunning, would lose him. Louise Fletcher meanwhile, was also proving potentially unavailable when her husband was forced to undergo emergency heart surgery.

During this time Rospo Pallenberg was still rewriting the ending for the movie, which involved the destruction of the original Georgetown house. However, as her patience had been severely tested by the amount of attention the first movie had brought to her property, Florence Mahoney refused permission for the production team to once again use her home as a central setting. Similarly, the city refused the film company permission to film on the Hitchcock steps. It was decided that the house and steps would also be built in Burbank. The studio was reportedly unhappy with this new ending and script supervisor Bonnie Prendergast proved most prescient when she took Pallenberg aside and told him that she thought the ending was now so full of disasters, it was almost a joke. Pallenberg and Boorman however opted to ignore this advice and ploughed on.

Filming resumed on 9 August, with the production relocating to New York shortly afterwards to shoot scenes in Regan's apartment, including her vertigo-inducing rooftop sleepwalk. (The Warner Communications building doubled as Regan's apartment block.) Goldwater Memorial Hospital, featured in several early scenes in the original movie, was another location used during this stage of filming.

Back In LA, the film production experienced further difficulties when certain scenes were over-developed by the lab, necessitating reshoots in New York; and Richard Burton, who married during the production, failed to turn up.

With time running out, Boorman was forced to trim his new ending. 2,500 male locusts – at a cost of $2 per bug – were shipped in from England for these climactic moments. One hundred of them arrived dead on delivery and they continued to die in the days to come at the rate of around one hundred a day. (Small pieces of polystyrene were eventually used in place of some of the insects.)

The final three weeks of the shoot was largely devoted to the destruction of the Georgetown house. However, the difficulties inherent in pulling off this complex sequence were exacerbated when Burton – present once again on set – announced that he had to leave on 1 November to begin filming *Equus*. Adding further grist to the curse of *The Exorcist* mill, Kitty Winn fell ill with a gall bladder infection, only to be followed by Louise Fletcher, who developed the very same ailment on her last day of filming. In addition to this, John

Merritt, the film's original editor, disappeared one day, having decided that he couldn't stand LA any longer and he decamped back to his native England.

"This whole film has been like animation," Boorman said as filming drew to a close. "We have been doing one frame at a time nearly. Not one thing could be taken for granted." The movie finally wrapped on 5 November 1976, several weeks later than expected, with Boorman retreating back to Ireland for post production.

At a final cost of $14 million, *Exorcist II: The Heretic* opened on 7 June 1977. Even before its release Bill Blatty felt that something was not quite right: "A couple of weeks before it was to open, I called Frank Wells at Warners," the author remembers. "I was living in Georgetown at the time and he said 'We'll be glad to set up a screening for you, Bill but please give me your word – a handshake agreement – if you don't like it, you won't go on television or to the press.' I said 'Hell, Frank, I can't do that. If it's really bad, don't show it to me.' He said 'I'll get back to you.' He didn't. So I paid my three, four dollars, went down to see it – unbelievable. Amazingly bad. Extraordinarily bad, if I remember. I called the producer Dick Lederer the next day and I said, 'Dick, I beg you, take the film out of release. Give it to me and, without touching a frame of the film, I will create an entirely new plot, new dialogue. It'll all be in subtitles or we'll dub it and pretend it's a foreign film, but it will be a comedy.' And I was dead serious. My favourite bit was when the cab driver gets out and runs over to Kitty Winn, and she's an ember, she's charred, her car has been burned to a crisp and she has also, and he says 'Are you alright?' I couldn't believe it."

Blatty admits he was the first person to start laughing in the theatre at which he saw the film, but was soon followed by the rest of the audience: "We roared from that point on – you'd think we were watching *The Producers*." The author was not alone in his assessment. Admittedly expectation was enormously high, but by any standards the reception awarded *Exorcist II,* by both the critics and the public alike, was unprecedented. Audiences were openly laughing at the movie during its New York première and sometimes the reaction was a little stronger.

"You know they rioted in the theatre where *Exorcist II* opened in Westwood, in Los Angeles," laughs Blatty. "And they called John Boorman over and I believe it was John Calley, the creative head at Warners, who personally took him to the theatre in the wee hours of the morning and showed him the destruction. They ripped the box office out of the ground; they tore the place apart. And Boorman, according to the reports, looked around and said 'Well, the film is obviously too good for them.'"

Boorman was quickly shipped back to the States. Within ten days of the film's release, he had prepared a new version. It was some fifteen minutes shorter and in it, Father Lamont appears to have died at the end, leaving Regan alone and triumphant against the forces of evil. Previously he had, literally, walked off into the morning light with her. Also added was a previously discarded voice-over prologue, while several other scenes were either trimmed or restructured. The new version of the movie was given another première on 17 June, eliciting a slightly better response, but by then there were 700 prints on release in the US and Warners had no desire to blow another million dollars on recalling them all and issuing new ones. The amended film was released in overseas markets but either way, the damage was already done.

"At the time I remember John Boorman saying 'I've re-dubbed everything. I've improved the performances one hundred per cent,'" says Blatty today. "I thought the performances were appalling. And that dialogue and that situation – 'I've flown this route before, on the wings of a locust' – Jesus!"

The movie proved to be a huge failure at the box office. "The sin I committed was not giving the audience what it wanted in terms of horror," Boorman said weakly in his defence at the time. "There's this wild beast out there which is the audience. I created this arena and I just didn't throw enough Christians into it. People think of cutting and re-cutting as defeat, but it isn't. As Irving Thalberg said: 'Films aren't made, they're remade.'"

In this case, they were unmade. *Exorcist II: The Heretic* remains one of the most notorious disasters in movie history. Who knows where the blame ultimately lies. Boorman's illness and constant revising of the script can't have helped, but these events alone are not enough to explain the film's almighty failure. Boorman has certainly gone on to produce some fine work subsequently.

When a list was compiled to find the fifty worst movies ever made, *Exorcist II: The Heretic* came in at number two. It was beaten only by Ed Wood's *Plan 9 From Outer Space*, a film that generally receives a warmer response from its audience than this terribly misjudged sequel.

"It was a really good script at first," Linda Blair recalled back in 1991. "Then after everybody signed on they rewrote it five times and it ended up nothing like the same movie. That was one of the big disappointments of my career."

Perhaps the final word on the film should come from the man who made the better, worthier original – Billy Friedkin: "I saw a half hour of it. I was at Technicolor and a guy said 'We just finished a print of *Exorcist II*, do you wanna have a look at it?' And I looked at a half hour of it and I thought it was as bad as seeing a traffic accident in the street. It was horrible. It's just a stupid mess made by a dumb guy – John Boorman by name, somebody who should be nameless but in this case he should be named. It's a travesty. Scurrilous. A horrible picture."

TWINKLE, TWINKLE, "KILLER" KANE –
THE NINTH CONFIGURATION

Despite his background as a successful comedy writer, *The Exorcist* had not been William Peter Blatty's first attempt at an exploration of his own faith. In 1966, Blatty published *Twinkle, Twinkle, "Killer" Kane*, an intriguing, sometimes comic, psychological piece which, in its brief, but telling theological discussions between characters, set up many of the themes that would later come to fruition in *The Exorcist*. Set in a mountain-bound military hospital, Kane focuses on a group of military men – an astronaut among them – all of whom have, in some way, been left traumatised in the line of duty. Through these men, Blatty explores the nature of madness and reality, faith and fear, good and evil.

"I considered it a comic novel," says Blatty "But a great deal of philosophy and theology crept into it along the way. But the farcical elements outweighed the more serious elements." Blatty later claimed that the book was written in haste and in 1978 he rewrote it as *The Ninth Configuration*. It was with this version that he would make his debut as film director.

"After *The Exorcist*," Blatty continues, "I decided that I could deepen the story a great deal. So I rewrote it and fleshed it out, and fully developed the deeper implications and the theological themes. As to which I prefer – the first one is infinitely funnier and wilder, and

William Peter Blatty

stranger and more of a one of a kind; the second one has the same plot, but the prose is more finely crafted, I think. In the first one I allowed the comedy to carry me, so I think I prefer that one. In some ways I prefer that book to *The Exorcist*. I loved the characters and it was pleasurable to write. *The Exorcist* was truly such hard work."

At this time, Blatty was not particularly enamoured of the studio system. In 1978, the author had sued Warner Brothers over his proper share of profits from *The Exorcist*. As producer he had originally been awarded 39 per cent of the movie's profits and had so far seen $17 million. He was now asking for a further $1.5 million in compensatory damages and $10 million in punitive damages. Furthermore, Blatty had written the screenplay for *The Ninth Configuration* for Columbia Pictures, who had then placed the movie in turnaround. "What happened after that is an illustration of how Hollywood works," the frustrated author said. "I then took the script to Universal and they rejected it, not because of any consideration of quality, but simply because Columbia had let it go. There was nobody prepared to take a chance on their own judgement."

So Blatty sought to finance *The Ninth Configuration*'s $4 million budget in a unique way: he put up half the money himself and persuaded mega-conglomerate Pepsi to put up the remaining $2 million. Pepsi thought they were on to a sure thing – after all, this was Blatty's first movie since he had written and produced one of the most successful pictures of all time – and the only restriction they placed on his creative control was that the movie had to be filmed in one of seven countries in which Pepsi had block funds. Consequently, the movie was shot in Hungary, where the money from the production was reinvested into the country in the form of a Pepsi bottling plant!

Furthering the film's ties with *The Exorcist*, Blatty cast Jason Miller, Ed Flanders (who had once been considered for the role of Karras) and Stacy Keach (who had originally lost out on the role of Father Karras to Miller) in the lead roles. (Scott Wilson and George DiCenzo, also cast, would later appear in *The Exorcist III* for Blatty, as would Flanders and Miller.) Blatty himself took a small role.

"I had cast Nicol Williamson in the role of Kane originally," recalls Blatty. "But I was deluding myself. I so desperately admired him and wanted him in my picture that I persuaded myself that he could be an American Marine Corps colonel. I realised during rehearsals. He was magnificent, but there was no way he could be an American colonel. He came to Budapest and we rehearsed for two weeks. And we were coming up to the weekend before our first shoot on the following Monday, and then I remembered one of the people I'd strongly considered was Stacy Keach. And we found out that night that he was available and he was with us on Tuesday."

Michael Moriarty was also dropped at this eleventh hour from the role of the astronaut, with Scott Wilson (already cast in another role) moving in to take over.

The darkly impressive psychological drama opened in 1980 to generally strong notices, but a poor box office. It originally appeared in a 105-minute cut, although Blatty himself prefers the 118-minute cut released in Europe. Despite the film's relative lack of success, Blatty went on to win an Academy Award nomination for his screenplay and he won that year's Golden Globe Award in the same category.

The Ninth Configuration was also nominated in the Best Picture category at the Golden Globes, but failed to secure a similar spot in that year's Oscar race, largely – Blatty believes – because of an article in the *Los Angeles Times* which claimed that the filmmaker had lavishly entertained members of the Foreign Press Association (those who award the Golden Globes) at his home. The truth was, having financed the movie largely by himself, Blatty used his home as a venue to screen it for the press: "I was even asked 'Did you serve them shrimp?' I swear to God."

LEGION – THE EXORCIST III

"I finally thought of a story that would make sense, years later," Bill Blatty explains of his eventual decision to pen a sequel to *The Exorcist*, "I loved the character of Kinderman and I wanted to see much more of him."

Published in 1983, *Legion* was the first true follow-up to *The Exorcist* and, along with *The Ninth Configuration*, it formed the third part of the author's unofficial faith trilogy. The novel focused on Lieutenant Kinderman's investigations into a baffling series of murders, all of which bear the hallmarks of a Georgetown serial murderer – the Gemini Killer – who had been killed by police twelve years before. Father Dyer, now a good cinema-going friend of the detective, was also a prominent figure in Blatty's novel.

Blatty began writing *Legion* as a screenplay and early on, had attracted Billy Friedkin to the project. Naturally, the thought of a genuine follow-up to *The Exorcist*, with the original talent attached, had every studio in Hollywood vying for its attention, with Warner Brothers going so far as to invite the writer and director to what Blatty refers to as "the half-million dollar lunch."

"Everybody wanted *Exorcist III*," says Blatty. "I hadn't written the script but I had the story in my head and Billy loved it, and our partner Jerry Weintraub loved it. Warner Brothers said 'Tell us the story'; we said 'No, we're not gonna tell you the story.' So they said 'Come to

New York, we'll have a little luncheon meeting and you tell us what you want of the story. Anything you want. And we'll either commit to make it based upon that or, if we don't like what you tell us, we're gonna give you half a million dollars.' The night before I typed it all up in a very neat form, ten or twelve pages, and I gave it to Jerry Weintraub. And Jerry was so excited. He said 'I'm gonna have these printed up, bind them in leather and I'm gonna put a copy in front of every Warner Brothers executive.' However, he gave it to Billy. Billy read it and, even though it was exactly what I'd told him, he invited me over to dinner at his apartment and he told me he didn't want to do it. He didn't like it. He said 'You're gonna have to cast Jason Miller. I don't want to work with Jason Miller. You've got people being beheaded, you've got knives in here – I did knives in *Cruising*. I don't want to do that. . .' He had eight million reasons and it was all, in my opinion, about not wanting to step up to bat again with an *Exorcist* title. So I said 'Then there's no meeting tomorrow, Billy.' But Jerry Weintraub physically took us down to the meeting. He said 'We're not passing up a half-million dollar lunch. This is absurd.' I said 'OK, but Billy, I'm not saying a word,' because Billy didn't want my outline presented. I said 'Billy, you talk, you tell them whatever you want to tell them.' So we sat down and Billy started to talk about an opening shot of mutilated cattle – I had never heard any of this. Billy is extremely articulate, but he went on about absolutely nothing. And my guess is that they loved it, but that night I backed out. I thought: Christ, Billy and I are not in agreement, we'll kill each other. I want to make *Legion*, Billy apparently doesn't want to make *Legion*. We got the money, split it three ways but I gave my money back. Looking back, I'd like to shoot that young man who turned down half a million dollars."

Having parted company with Friedkin, Blatty then decided to write *Legion* as a novel. Published in 1983, it went on to become a bestseller: "In *The Exorcist*, questions were raised regarding God's providence and goodness," Blatty explained of his novel. "In *Legion*, there is a presentation of a possible solution to the problem of evil, with which I can certainly find – if you grant my premises – no fault. It preserves the goodness of God, while not denying evil."

By the end of the decade, Blatty had turned *Legion* back into a screenplay, which was sought by two major companies – Carolco and Morgan Creek. When Carolco suggested a new plot twist – Kinderman's daughter should become possessed – Blatty opted to go with Morgan Creek. There were two further stipulations to Blatty's deal. First, that he should direct and second, that the movie be filmed on location back in Georgetown: "Thrillers depend on credibility," he explained. "Georgetown has a look like no other place in the world. We had to film in Georgetown – not on the backlot – or the picture could not be made. Not by me."

Early on, Blatty defined what he saw as the unique qualities of his movie: "Where it really differs from *The Exorcist* is in the way it's made. This is my idea of terror, this is what frightens me – creaks and shadows, not turning heads and all the rest – which have their place, but not in this film. I think we've all understood that your imagination can do more to terrify you than anything presented to you graphically, and that is particularly true today, when audiences are so numbed by everything they've seen that young people are actually laughing at scenes of bloodshed and decapitation. But if you manipulate their deepest fears through suggestion, it will terrify an audience more than specific gore."

Having lost Lee J. Cobb, Blatty cast Oscar winner George C. Scott in the lead role of Kinderman. Having never seen the original movie, Scott thought the script was the scariest thing he'd read in over thirty years: "It's a horror film and much more," he said "It's a real drama, intricately crafted, with offbeat interesting characters, and that's what makes it so genuinely frightening."

Ed Flanders took up the role of Father Dyer, while *Ninth Configuration* alumni Scott Wilson and George DiCenzo were also on board, as was Jason Miller, reprising his role as Damien Karras (although billed as 'Patient X'). Brad Dourif rounded off the cast as the Gemini Killer.

Budgeted at $11 million, shooting began on location in Georgetown in May 1989. After eight weeks, the production relocated to the DEG Studios in Wilmington, North Carolina for additional interiors. As ever, Blatty found that some people were wary of connecting themselves with anything that had a certain word in the title: "Our effects co-ordinator received a call from the owner of a cobra named Joe, we were using in one sequence and he said 'Look, I'm sorry about this. The money is good, and it's a swell opportunity in every other way, but my wife and I talked this through, looking at all sides of it, and we both felt we really don't want Joe to be in an *Exorcist* film.' What must the reputation of the film be?"

Blatty brought the movie in on time, marginally over budget, at a final cost of $12 million. Four months after principal photography however, he was called back to film a new ending for the movie. "James Robinson, the owner of the company, his secretary had insisted to him that this has nothing to do with *The Exorcist*. There had to be an exorcism."

At the time Blatty insisted to the press that he was happy to have this opportunity to provide the film with a dazzling, effects-laden finale, which saw Nicol Williamson (late of *The Ninth Configuration*) cast as Father Morning. "Quite frankly, at the time we were shooting," he bluffed to *Fear* magazine "I hadn't dreamed up the scene yet or the effects. So I said 'Until I think of the right thing, it's not in the picture.' I'm trying for effects we've never seen before, not the usual. We're spending a lot of money – a lot. Over $4 million. We're going to repeat everything that was in *The Exorcist*. The scene will be infinitely shorter; it will be compacted into a very brief period of time so the effects will come at you like dumdum bullets."

In reality, this compromised ending was forced on Blatty by Morgan Creek. "I agreed to film it because it was either me or them," he now explains. "The original story that I sold them (and that I shot) ended with Kinderman blowing away Patient X. There was no exorcism. But it was a Mexican stand-off between me and the studio. I was entitled to one preview, then they could go and do what they wanted with the picture. They gave me a preview but it was the lowest end preview audience I have ever seen in my life. They dragged in zombies from Haiti to watch this film. It was unbelievable.

But I decided, better I should do it than anyone else. I foolishly thought: I can do a good exorcism. I'll turn this pig's ear into a silk purse. So I did it. It's alright, but it's utterly unnecessary and it changes the character of the piece."

Despite this compromise the movie was generally well received by the critics on its release, although its box-office life proved short-lived, largely – Blatty believes – due to the film's title, which at various times was called *Exorcist: 1990*, *Exorcist: Fifteen Years Later*, *Exorcist: A New Chapter* and *Exorcist: Legion*. Blatty had originally wanted to simply retain the name '*Legion*', but Morgan Creek insisted on getting the word '*Exorcist*' into the title: "They promised me they would never do that. I begged them when they were considering titles not to name it '*Exorcist*' anything, because *Exorcist II* was a disaster beyond imagination. You can't call it *Exorcist III* because people will shun the box office. But they went and named it *Exorcist III*, then they called me after the third week when we were beginning to fade at the box office and they said 'We'll tell you the reason, it's gonna hurt, you're not gonna like this – the reason is *Exorcist II*.' I couldn't believe it. They have total amnesia." Nonetheless, Blatty remains proud of his movie today: "It's still a superior film. And in my opinion, and excuse me if I utter heresy here, but for me it's a more frightening film than *The Exorcist*."

CHAPTER TWENTY

THE PARODIES

The *Exorcist* remains one of the most parodied movies of all time. From the image of Father Merrin's arrival at the MacNeil house to the possessed Regan, the film has been lampooned by everyone from the Simpsons to French and Saunders, and beyond. And finding a TV game show host who delivers the line: "Your mother darns socks in hell" is not unheard of.

Two of the more interesting of these parodies both featured Linda Blair, sending up her most famous role. The first of these, however – *The Heckling* – remains largely unseen. In 1987, writer-director Bryan Michael Stoller was working on a movie called *Undershorts* for Paramount Pictures. *Undershorts* was intended as a *Kentucky Fried Movie* style collection of sketches and skits, one of which was a seven-minute send-up of *The Exorcist*. In it, Linda Blair plays both the mother and daughter roles, the latter 'possessed' by the spirit of any number of comedians, from Steve Martin to Jack Benny, and beyond. The Rabbi that comes to exorcise her proves ineffective and the 'demon comics' can only be driven out by two beer-guzzling hecklers, dragged in from a nearby comedy club: "I had never actually seen *The Exorcist*, but I wanted to spoof all the famous classic movies," says Stoller. "So I rented *The Exorcist* for the first time and somebody I knew, knew Linda Blair and introduced me to her. And she really liked the project, and turned down other stuff to do with *The Exorcist* because she didn't really want to be connected to that. But she really liked this spoof and she agreed to do it."

Blair had a thoroughly good time sending up her most successful role, although according to Stoller, she had some help with the voices: "We had voice impersonators do people like Robin Williams, Joan Rivers, PeeWee Herman, Steve Martin, and she had to lip synch to those voices. We had playback on the set and she was very good."

Due to a change of power at Paramount, *Undershorts* was unfortunately never released, but it did serve to inspire another parody. Bob Logan was a friend of Linda Blair who had seen the film and, when he heard that it wasn't going to be released, he decided to pitch the idea as a feature. The result was *Repossessed*. "He took it to a smaller studio," says Stoller "And they said 'If you can get Linda Blair, we'll do it.' And they paid her $800,000 to do it, so I don't blame her for not turning it down."

Logan wrote the screenplay for Blair, but the actress was at first reluctant to do it. "He said to me 'What would it take for you to do it?' And I said 'Leslie Nielsen.' So they came round, saying they'd got Leslie and I agreed."

Despite having spent the vast majority of his career as a conventional straight-character actor, since the 1980 success of *Airplane*, Nielsen had become synonymous with broad Hollywood parody. (Interestingly, Blair's role of the girl awaiting a kidney transplant being tended to by a singing nun in *Airport '75* was wickedly spoofed in *Airplane*. Blair herself had wanted to play the role, but was restricted on contractural grounds.)

Logan's film effectively sent up many elements from Friedkin and Blatty's classic, but when younger test audiences proved to be not up to speed on *The Exorcist*, the film was radically re-shot and re-edited to accommodate numerous other sketches and references: "The whole thing needed to be shortened," Blair explained back in 1991 "And then you needed material to bridge the gaps. Bob Logan trod a very thin line between drama and comedy; some of it wasn't funny, it came across as serious. So they went back and added jokes and also added that musical sequence at the end, 'Devil In A Blue

Dress', which was supposed to be a video release, but it never happened."

The film suffered significantly on its American release, something that wasn't helped by *The Exorcist III*, as Blair explained to *The Dark Side* magazine: "We were doing press for an August release date and the next thing we knew *The Exorcist III* was coming out within a week of us. So they jumped on our bandwagon with the publicity; they weren't due out for release for two months, but they rushed it out and got it into theatres and everyone thought that was my movie. People just confused it. In Texas and North Carolina, the films actually came out together and people didn't know which movie they were going to see. People who wanted to see *The Exorcist III* saw *Repossessed* and were saying 'But I wanted to see a drama.' And people who wanted to see *Repossessed* saw *The Exorcist III* and said 'Where's Linda Blair?' So it got really confusing and in the end they pulled the release for the East Coast because they said it would cost them 10 to 20 million dollars more to alter the advertising so people knew the difference."

Repossessed was also forced to carry the following declaration on all its advertising: "This motion picture parody is in no way connected to the makers or writers of *The Exorcist* or any of its sequels." The film was a failure at the box office.

THE EXORCIST TODAY

On Halloween weekend 1998, *The Exorcist* was re-released in the UK to celebrate the film's twenty-fifth anniversary. Over the weekend, this quarter-century old movie grossed over £2 million, becoming the number one film throughout the land. That first night two ambulances were called to screenings in London to deal with reported faintings.

Undoubtedly, one of the reasons for the film's huge success in the UK was the fact of its unavailability. Under the Video Recordings Act, it had effectively been banned on video for the best part of a decade. In the July 1998 issue of *Sight and Sound*, James Ferman, the soon-to-retire head of the British Board of Film Classification (BBFC), outlined his reasons for the film's continued absence on British video shelves: "The problem with *The Exorcist* is not that it's a bad film, it's that it's a very good film – one of the most powerful films ever made – and it's that power which is a problem on video. The amended Video Recordings Act says the BBFC should have special regard to the harm that could be caused to potential viewers – including under-age viewers – because of the manner in which a video deals with, among other things, horror. *The Exorcist* is of particular interest to young teenagers because its protagonist is twelve years old. A lot of teenage girls are going to want to see it and will identify with Regan, who is subject to probably the most intense terrorisation on film.

"We know that when *The Exorcist* came out there were a lot of traumatised teenage girls being helped out of the cinema. We consulted two child psychiatrists who said that the film was, in their view, extraordinarily powerful, particularly to young teenage girls, who were susceptible to being convinced that evil is a real presence in the world. We also know that religious imagery is powerful to girls of around twelve to fifteen. Most people who practise religion talk about an all-seeing, benevolent God; few any longer talk about a force of evil. But this film treats it seriously because Blatty was writing a religious film, which Friedkin made into one of the great horror films. The power of religion is there. It's not a Freddy Krueger; it doesn't operate on that shoddy, superficial level.

"Our problem, therefore, has nothing to do with thinking there's anything wrong with the film. I think it's a wonderful film for adults. But video is a different medium and there are some films we think are not very suitable for viewing in the home. And I don't believe in cutting very good films simply to get them on to video.

"We've gone through periods when all the examiners have seen *The Exorcist* and written reports, and many of those reports say this film is simply too powerful and too scary, though some examiners have argued that it's time to pass it. We now have a completely new set of examiners and a new president, who has the casting vote. All we can do is make the best decision we can this week. But I can't vouch for what might happen next year."

"I can understand it on the one hand," Friedkin says in reply to Ferman. "Ferman's statement says: 'We're not denying the film a certificate because it's a bad film; we're denying it a certificate because it's too good. It's too powerful.' That's where I take issue with him. That's censorship. 'We're not denying this man television time because we think he's a bad man. We're denying him television time because we don't like his ideas.' Now that is real censorship and also it treats audiences like children. It's saying to the British public: 'You people are too stupid to really know how to react to this film or to even accept the premise that it is just a film, so we can't let you see it.' In terms of children seeing it, of course I can understand that there should be some limitation and restriction, but it should be parental. Again, it's saying to the parents of children that: 'You people are not responsible enough to take care of your own children in terms of what goes into their minds. You're too stupid or you don't care, so we're gonna do it for you. The State is gonna tell you what you should expose your children to. We're not gonna say to you show them whatever you want, but discuss it with them. Or don't show it to them, it's your choice. We're gonna make the choice for you – what should be seen and what shouldn't,' and that's censorship. There are many people, of course who are without children and they're denied seeing it on television and video as well. They're being told they're too susceptible, they're too dumb, they're all gonna turn into demons if they see this picture, or they're gonna go out and kill somebody or do something stupid if they see this picture. On the one hand, it's censorship; on the other hand, it's treating the great British public like a bunch of childish dolts that need to be protected from their own devices. I can certainly understand the impulse to keep this from children. I cannot understand the impulse to keep it from adults. The book isn't banned. How did they miss that? That's the source.

"Over the years a lot of stupid opinions were heard in England. Oswald Mosely, Enoch Powell and a great many others were allowed to go out there because they had power, or position or high office, and spout the most nonsensical things imaginable. Now with these other media, the censors have moved in and you can't do this, you can't show that, you mustn't say this. I now realise what a powerful effect the film has after twenty-five years. Is it possible that some people would see the film and do something terrible? I suppose it's possible – yes, so I can understand the impulse. But I really do think it's infantalising the British public."

Censorship or not, the fact is that twenty-five years after the film's original release, it retains a power that is unique in all of cinema. It certainly proved to be a yardstick for its principal players to measure their subsequent careers against.

William Friedkin received his second Oscar nomination as Best Director for *The Exorcist*. Having made both that and *The French Connection* back-to-back, Friedkin's subsequent career has proved to be often erratic, ranging from such visually impressive works as his *Wages Of Fear* remake *Sorcerer,* through the controversy of the Al Pacino-led *Cruising,* to the impressive and stylish action of *To Live And Die In LA*. Along the way however, there have been a number of lesser efforts including the lamentable Joe Eszterhas-penned thriller *Jade* in 1995, the mid-eighties TV show *C.A.T. Squad* and the director's return to the horror genre, 1990's possessed tree number *The Guardian*. However, Friedkin's most recent work saw him back on good form, with a George C. Scott led remake of *12 Angry Men* for American cable TV.

Following her Oscar nomination for *The Exorcist*, Linda Blair went on to star in a vast number of movies, many of them exploitational in nature, generally finding themselves filed under the 'straight-to-video' category. She attracted good notices for her starring role in the TV movie *Sarah T: Portrait Of A Teenage Alcoholic*, did star turns in the all-star ensembles of *Airport '75* and *Victory At Entebbe*, and won teenage hearts as the star of the feelgood movie *Roller Boogie*. But for well over a decade after that, Ms Blair's work was generally to be seen opposite the likes of Sylvia (*Emmanuelle*) Kristel and Wings Hauser in such titles as *Red Heat*, *Chained Heat*, *Bad Blood*, *Dead Sleep*, *Savage Streets* and *Hell Night*.

The fact that most of these movies were actually better than *Exorcist II* is neither here nor there. Blair's reputation as Regan and a steady number of genre appearances assured the actress a cult following throughout the eighties, but her hopes that *Repossessed* would, once and for all, bury the spirit of Pazuzu sadly proved not to be the case. "You want to say 'When will it end? When will they stop asking me about it?' " she confided to the *Evening Standard* in late 1998. "What am I in? *The Twilight Zone*? At the same time you are also aware that you are part of something that has affected the whole world. But that was never my idea – that was Billy Friedkin's idea. I was just a young girl, playing with the boys, watching the boys play. That was what it looked like from where I was on the bed. You know they say you're never given more than you can handle? Well, I always felt I was given an awful lot. Many times I felt I was carrying a cross, trying to answer people's questions, being bombarded, judged, ridiculed."

Blair's private life continued to be the stuff of tabloid headlines when the FBI were called in to protect her, following death threats from a man who believed she was a nymphomaniac possessed by the Devil. The FBI cropped up again in her life when they tapped her phone, suspecting her of conspiring to sell cocaine. (She was fined and placed on probation.)

A co-starring role as Rizzo in the Broadway revival of *Grease* in 1997 saw Blair draw rave notices and finally – hopefully – lay the ghost of Regan to rest. She is currently developing her own sitcom.

Max von Sydow's appearance in *The Exorcist* served to introduce him to a far wider audience than either his earlier acclaimed pairings with Ingmar Bergman or his occasional English language movie appearances. For his subsequent career, the actor would divide his time between delivering award-worthy performances in such American fare as Woody Allen's *Hannah And Her Sisters* and award-winning performances in acclaimed European productions such as *Pelle The Conqueror*. In a career that can be easily be described as 'diverse', von Sydow has also found time to play Ming The Merciless in 1980's *Flash Gordon*, a future Judge in 1995's *Judge Dredd* and a football-loving Nazi in John Huston's lamentable *Escape To Victory*.

Ellen Burstyn, like Billy Friedkin, also picked up her second Oscar nomination with *The Exorcist*, although she failed to win that year. This was rectified the following season when she walked away with the Best Actress statuette for her titular role in Martin Scorsese's *Alice Doesn't Live Here Anymore*. She began the following decade on another high note with yet another nomination, this time for *Resurrection*. Since then however, Burstyn seems to have fallen prey to that Hollywood maxim that there are no decent roles for 'women of a certain age', being forced to deliver small roles in increasingly minor movies such as *Dying Young*, *The Spitfire Grill* and *Liar*.

Jason Miller performed a unique double in the year he made *The Exorcist*. He was Oscar-nominated as Best Supporting Actor and he won the Pulitzer Prize for literature for his play *That Championship Season*. He also picked up a Tony Award, a Drama Circle Critics Award and an Outer Circle Critics Award in the same year – a championship season, indeed. (He directed the movie version of his play in 1982.) Miller has subsequently divided his career between acting and writing. His on-screen career has often proved to be erratic and unsatisfying, appearing in such movies as Paul Schrader's *Light Of Day* and alongside Christopher Reeve in the religious thriller *Monsignor*, although his role on TV in *F. Scott Fitzgerald In Hollywood* did land the actor an Emmy nomination.

In 1986, Miller returned to his home town of Scranton, Pennsylvania, to take up the post of artistic director of the Scranton Public Theatre, for whom he has penned and staged a number of works. "It got me here with this theatre," Miller now says of his involvement with the most frightening film ever made. "I consider myself more of a theatre man than I do a movie man, but it undoubtedly altered my life and brought a sea change into my life. I'm just glad it brought me here, where I can do my plays." (Miller's son is the actor Jason Patrick.)

William Peter Blatty, more than anyone else, has lived with the spectre of his most successful work. The popularity and impact of the novel and the film of *The Exorcist* effectively ended Blatty's career in comedy, although in 1996 he attempted to address this issue by subverting the legends and the myth of *The Exorcist* with his hugely enjoyable comic novel *Demons Five, Exorcists Nothing*. Anyone with even a passing knowledge or interest in the movie can see the parallels in Blatty's tale of filmmaker Jason Hazard as he makes a movie of the bestselling *The Satanist*. (Shirley MacLaine and Warren Beatty dopplegangers also crop up, if you know where to find them.) "My motivation was to bemuse the reader," Blatty explains. "*Demons Five...* is what I used to write in novel after novel before *The Exorcist*. Now that's exactly what nobody wants me to do. Their eyes glaze over if you say my name and comedy. It absolutely drives me crazy. I have this quote on my desk from the *New York Times* because even I stopped believing it and it says 'Nobody can write funnier lines than William Peter Blatty.' Goodbye to that life!"

In 1997, Blatty returned to his novel once more and adapted *The Exorcist* into a proposed four-hour TV mini series for Fox TV: "I did the four-hour adaptation so I could do the whole novel. I wanted all the theology to be in there. I'm rather pleased with it. Peter Fonda was dying to do it, to play Merrin. But it's not happening anymore."

Fox's unwillingness to give the production a decent budget would have meant that location work in Georgetown would have been impossible. Moreover, Blatty was none too happy with Fox's casting suggestion for the key role of Lt Kinderman – Rosie O'Donnell, Whoopi Goldberg or Queen Latifah!

There is an *Exorcist IV* planned – rumoured to deal once again with Father Merrin's first battle with Pazuzu in Africa – but Blatty is not involved. And in 1998, a possible weekly television show, *The Exorcist – The Series*, much in the style of the popular straight-to-syndication *Poltergeist – The Legacy*, seems to be on the cards. Once again, Blatty is in no way involved. Instead, the author continues to work on a new novel, a theological thriller called *Dimiter* that he has now been working on for just over a decade.

"I've always said that you get from the film what you bring to it," says Billy Friedkin today. "If you think the world is shit, ultimately and basically, you look at *The Exorcist* and say 'Right, that's what I told you, the world is shit. The Devil can enter someone's life at will and destroy it.' If you think, on the other hand, that the world is full of hope and potential, and possibility and redemption and cure from pain, then you take that from *The Exorcist*. That's what I take from it – always did. The biggest surprise was that a lot of people took the opposite. There is no resolution. The human soul is a battlefield, a continuous battlefield for good and evil on a day-to-day, almost hour-by-hour basis."

Horror films traditionally offer their audience a kind of catharsis. In the mid-nineties Wes Craven reinvented the genre with the *Scream* movies, based on that simple premise: you come, you watch, you scream. It's fun. *The Exorcist*, which in its simplest description is a horror movie, although it is so much more, doesn't offer that. Yes, good does win over evil in the end, but there's no release. Perhaps that's why, twenty-five years later, it still scares and stuns its audience. In that way, it has possessed us all.

And perhaps ultimately, for the people who made it, the real curse of *The Exorcist* is that for them too, there is no release. Says William Peter Blatty: "I remember years ago my good friend Mario Puzo remarked to me very casually 'You know, people ask me what business I'm in when I meet them. And you know, I always say I'm in the *Godfather* business.' Well, I guess I turned out to be in *The Exorcist* business."

FILMOGRAPHIES: LIFE AFTER THE EXORCIST

WILLIAM PETER BLATTY

The Ninth Configuration (1980
– from his own novel; also
actor, director and producer)
The Exorcist III (1990 – from
own his novel, *Legion*; also
director)

WILLIAM FRIEDKIN

Sorcerer (1977)
The Brink's Job (1978)
Cruising (1980)
Deal Of The Century (1983)
To Live And Die In L.A. (1985)
C.A.T. Squad (TV 1986)
Rampage (1987)
The Guardian (1990)
Blue Chips (1994)
Jade (1995)
Twelve Angry Men (TV 1997)

MAX VON SYDOW

Steppenwolf (1974)
Egg! Egg! A Hard-boiled Story
(1974)
Foxtrot/The Other Side Of
Paradise (1975)
The New Land (1975)
Il Contesto (1975)
Cuore Di Cane (1975)
Three Days Of The Condor
(1975)
Illustrious Corpses (1976)
Voyage Of The Damned (1976)
The Ultimate Warrior (1976)
Les Desert Des Tartares (1976)
Exorcist II: The Heretic (1977)
March Or Die (1977)
La Signora Della Orrori (1977)
Gran Bollito (1978)
Brass Target (1978)
Hurricane (1979)
La Mort En Direct/Deathwatch
(1979)
A Look At Liv (1979)
Flash Gordon (1980)
She Dances Alone (1980)
Bugie Bianchi (1980)
Flight Of The Eagle (1981)
Escape To Victory (1981)
Conan The Barbarian (1982)
Strange Brew (1983)
Never Say Never Again (1983)
Cercel Des Passions (1983)
Dreamscape (1984)
Dune (1984)
Samson And Delilah (TV 1984)
The Ice Pirates (TV 1984)
Kojak: The Belarus File (TV
1985)
Christopher Columbus (TV
1985)
Code Name: Emerald (1985)
The Last Place On Earth (TV
1985)
Quo Vadis (TV 1985)
The Wolf At The Door (1986)
The Second Victory (1986)
Duet For One (1986)
Hannah And Her Sisters (1986)

Pelle The Conqueror (1987)
Katinka (1988 – director)
Red King, White Knight (TV 1989)
My Dear Doctor Grasler (1990)
Awakenings (1990)
Father (1990)
Violent Life (1990)
Hiroshima: Out Of The Ashes (1990)
A Kiss Before Dying (1991)
Until The End Of The World (1991)
The Bachelor (1991)
The Ox (1991)
Europa (1992)
The Best Intentions (1992)
Silent Touch (1993)
Morfars Resa (1993)
Needful Things (1993)
Time Is Money (1994)
Judge Dredd (1995)
Atlanten (1995)
Citizen X (TV 1995)
Jerusalem (1996)
Hansum (1996)

ELLEN BURSTYN

Harry And Tonto (1974)
Thursday's Game (TV 1974)
Alice Doesn't Live Here Anymore (1975)
Providence (1977)
A Dream Of Passion (1978)
Same Time, Next Year (1978)
Resurrection (1980)
Silence Of The North (1982)

The People Versus Jean Harris (TV 1983)
The Ambassador (1984)
Surviving (TV 1985)
Twice In A Lifetime (1985)
Into Thin Air (TV 1985)
Something In Common (TV 1986)
Dear America (1987)
Hello Actors Studios (1987)
Pack Of Lies (TV 1987)
Hanna's War (1988)
Act Of Vengeance – A True Story (TV 1989)
The Color Of Evening (1990)
When You Remember Me (TV 1990)
Dying Young (1991)
Mrs Lambert Remembers Love (TV 1991)
Grand Isle (TV 1992)
Taking Back My Life (TV 1992)
The Cemetery Club (1993)
Shattered Trust: The Shari Karney Story (TV 1993)
When A Man Loves A Woman (1994)
Getting Out (TV 1994)
Getting Gotti (TV 1994)
Trick Of The Eye (TV 1994)
The Baby-Sitters' Club (1995)
How To Make An American Quilt (1995)
My Brother's Keeper (TV 1995)
Follow The River (TV 1995)
The Spitfire Gill (1996)
Liar (1997)

JASON MILLER

The Nickel Ride (1974)

A Home Of Our Own (TV 1976)

F. Scott Fitzgerald In Hollywood (TV 1976)

The Dain Curse (TV 1978)

The Devil's Advocate (1979)

Vampire (1979)

Marilyn: The Untold Story (1980)

The Ninth Configuration (1980)

The Henderson Monster (TV 1980)

The Best Little Girl In The World (TV 1981)

That Championship Season (1982 – writer/director)

Monsignor (1982)

Toy Soldiers (1984)

A Touch Of Scandal (TV 1984)

Light Of Day (1987)

The Exorcist III (1990)

Deadly Care (TV 1992)

Rudy (1993)

LINDA BLAIR (selected)

Born Innocent (TV 1974)

Airport '75 (1975)

Sarah T – Portrait of a Teenage Alcoholic (TV 1975)

Sweet Hostage (TV 1975)

The Art Of Crime (TV 1975)

Victory At Entebbe (TV 1976)

Exorcist II: The Heretic (1977)

Stranger In Our House (TV 1978)

Wild Horse Hank (1978)

Hard Ride To Rantan (1979)

Roller Boogie (1979)

Hell Night (1981)

Ruckus (1984)

Savage Streets (1984)

Chained Heat (1985)

Night Patrol (1985)

Red Heat (1985)

Illusions (1985)

Savage Island (1985)

Night Force (1986)

Silent Assassins (1987)

Undershorts – The Movie (1987 – unreleased)

Grotesque (1988)

Bad Blood/A Woman Obsessed (1989)

The Chilling (1989)

Moving Target (1989)

Zapped Again (1989)

Bail Out (1989)

Bedroom Eyes II (1989)

Up Your Alley (1989)

Witchery/Ghosthouse II (1989)

Dead Sleep (1990)

Repossessed (1990)

House 5 (1991)

The Fatal Bond (1991)

Beyond Control (1991)

Sorceress (1994)

Skins (1995)

Dead Sleep (1995)

Prey Of The Jaguar (1996)

Gang Boys (1997)

BIBLIOGRAPHY

Biskind, Peter: Easy Riders,
Raging Bulls
(New York, Simon & Schuster,
1998)
Blatty, William Peter:
The Exorcist (New York, Harper
& Rowe, 1971);
Twinkle Twinkle "Killer" Kane
(London, Futura, 1975);
The Ninth Configuration (New
York, Bantam, 1978);
Legion (New York, Bantam,
1974);
Demons Five, Exorcists Nothing
(New York, Donald J. Fine
Books, 1996);
On The Exorcist: From Novel To
Film (New York, Bantam, 1974)
Kermode, Mark: BFI Modern
Classics: The Exorcist
(London, BFI, 1997)
Wilson Bryan Key: Media
Sexploitation
(New Jersey, Prentice Hall Inc.,
1976)
Newman, Howard: The
Exorcist: The Strange Story
Behind The Film (New York,
Pinnacle Books, 1974)
Pallenberg, Barbara: The
Making Of Exorcist II: The
Heretic
(New York, Bantam, 1977)
Segaloff, Nat: Hurricane Billy
(New York, William
Morrow, 1990)
Travers, Peter & Stephanie
Reiff: The Story Behind The
Exorcist
(New York, New American
Library, 1974)

SOURCES
American Cinematographer,
Castle Of Frankenstein,
Cinefantastique, Cineaste,
Empire, Fangoria, Fear, Film
Criticism, Literature and Film
Quarterly, Monthly Film
Bulletin, Movie, Newsweek,
Photon, Samhain, Screen
International, Sight And Sound,
Speakeasy, The Daily
Telegraph, The Dark Side, The
Evening Standard, The
Guardian, The Independent,
The New York Times, The
Times, The Washington Post,
Time Out, 20/20, Variety,
Velvet Light Trap, Video
Watchdog

TELEVISION
Freand Jones, Nick (Producer):
The Fear of God: 25 Years Of
The Exorcist (BBC documen-
tary)